APPROACHING THE MYSTERY OF GOLGOTHA

RUDOLF STEINER (1913)

APPROACHING THE MYSTERY OF GOLGOTHA

Ten Lectures Held in Various Cities in 1913-14

Translated by Michael Miller

Introduction by Christopher Bamford

RUDOLF STEINER

SteinerBooks

CW 152

SteinerBooks
Anthroposophic Press

P.O. Box 58
Hudson, New York 12534
www.steinerbooks.org

Original translation from the German by Michael Miller

This book is volume 152 in the Collected Works (CW) of Rudolf Steiner, published by SteinerBooks, 2006. It is a translation of the German *Vorstufen zum Mysterium von Golgatha*, published by Rudolf Steiner Verlag, Dornach, Switzerland, 1986.

Library of Congress Cataloging-in-Publication Data

Steiner, Rudolf, 1861-1925.
[Vorstufen zum Mysterium von Golgatha. English]
Approaching the mystery of Golgotha : ten lectures held in various cities in 1913-14 / Rudolf Steiner ; translated by Michael Miller ; introduction by Christopher Bamford.
p. cm. — (Collected works of Rudolf Steiner ; v. 152)
Includes bibliographical references and index.
ISBN 0-88010-606-9
1. Anthroposophy. 2. Jesus Christ—Miscellanea. I. Title.

BP595.S894V6813 2006
299'.935--dc22
2006021272

Printed in the United States

CONTENTS

INTRODUCTION

CHRISTOPHER BAMFORD

1913 (the year most of the lectures collected here were given) was historically critical for the Western world in general and Rudolf Steiner and Anthroposophy in particular. Spiritual realities—creative and destructive—were busy behind the scenes. The Great War had already cast its shadow onto the earthly stage. Eighteen months later, it would erupt, producing in its wake four years of human suffering and carnage. Almost ten million people, six thousand a day, would perish; and, with them, a world would disappear. Rudolf Steiner was not alone in sensing the approaching change and preparing for it in various ways.

During this period, as part of the general transformation underway, the spiritual context of Anthroposophy (and Theosophy) was also preparing to change. 1913 would be a landmark year for Rudolf Steiner and Anthroposophy. For the past decade, Anthroposophy had sat fruitfully but uneasily—a little like the grain of sand in the proverbial oyster that would produce the pearl—within the mother-womb of Theosophy. In the darkening months of world evolution leading to war, it would pass a significant milestone in its incarnation, separating from Theosophy to become an independent spiritual impulse.

On February 3, 1913, after a year or more of gestation, the first General Meeting of the Anthroposophical Society was held. In September, the Foundation Stone for the Goetheanum was laid in Dornach. The ground for Anthroposophy as we know it today was established. The separation from Theosophy, it must be said, was a double-edged sword. It cut both ways. While Anthroposophy certainly gained immeasurably in depth, intensity, and clarity of purpose, it also perhaps lost something of its planetary context. It became inevitably more Euro- and even Germano-centric. Perhaps every gain in depth is a loss of breadth. Theosophy, for its part, was severely diminished. Split, losing its evolutionary thrust, in some sense it never recovered.

Rudolf Steiner's relationship with the Theosophical Society, while necessary because (as he said) of "deep underlying causes," had always been difficult and filled with tensions. From the beginning (1902), though deeply grateful for the opportunity to work within the movement inaugurated through Madame Blavatsky and genuinely dedicated to its ideals and principles, Steiner had taught always and only from his own experience, seeing as his mission the bringing of a contemporary, future-oriented Western-Christian impulse into Theosophy's predominantly static—because essentially anti-Judaeo-Christian—Indian (Buddhist and Hindu) framework. Not that he did so in any sense in opposition to Theosophy. Quite the contrary, he felt that he was responding to the inner needs of the Theosophical Movement itself, and that Madame Blavatsky herself was blessing his initiative. But it is always difficult to bring something new into a movement that has become more or less ideological and fixed in its ways. There is always resistance, based on fear and ignorance. Power challenged, feels threatened and, no matter how "spiritual," politics as usual is the result.

The tensions implicit in this undertaking—at work beneath the surface from the beginning—began to come to a head in 1906-7 with the forced resignation of the former Anglican clergyman, prolific theosophical author, and accomplished clairvoyant, Charles Leadbeater (1854-1934) for sexual misconduct with young boys. (He was teaching them to masturbate.) For Steiner, Leadbeater's "moral lapse" was a consequence of his *occult methods*, which, from Steiner's point of view, were "dangerous and apt to mislead." As he wrote to Annie Besant:

> I have to see the cause of all this misfortune in the peculiarity of Mr. Leadbeater's occult methods. These occult methods necessarily lead, in certain cases, to this or other mistakes similar to those evinced in Mr. Leadbeater's case, because such methods are no longer appropriate to the current stage of Western humanity.... These methods can only lead to positive results if, standing behind everyone who enters on the path of development, there is the absolute authority of the guru—which is impossible in the West

> due to the general cultural situation. Western people can be led to the stage of psychic development where Leadbeater stood only if the part of their guidance that can no longer proceed from the guru is replaced by a *mental development* that has reached a certain stage.... In Germany, for example, the way to this kind of learning must be taken from the thought-mysticism of Fichte, Schelling, and Hegel....

Without such mental development, Steiner continues, Westerners "wander about without a rudder," ignorant of what plane they are on.

The immediate upshot was that Leadbeater resigned from the Theosophical Society. As to the question of what path was appropriate for humanity, prior to and during the international Munich Theosophical Congress of 1907, which demonstrated in the strongest manner the Rosicrucian basis of Steiner's teaching, Annie Besant was forced to acknowledge her incompetence with regard to Christianity and—apparently magnanimously—accept Steiner's primacy in this area. She wrote:

> Dr. Steiner's occult training is very different from ours. He does not know the Eastern way, so cannot, of course, teach it. He teaches the Christian and Rosicrucian way, and this is very helpful to some, but is different from ours. I regard him as a very fine teacher on his own lines, and also a man of real knowledge. He and I work through friendship and harmony, but along different lines.

Accordingly, Rudolf Steiner gained permission to separate his Esoteric Section of the Germany Society from the general Esoteric Section—that is, to teach the Western way to Westerners. With Besant's blessing, two Esoteric Sections were thus established: an Eastern School and a Western, essentially Rosicrucian, School, to be established and guided by Rudolf Steiner.

Leadbeater's decisive, indeed karmic, role, however, was by no means over. His connection with Besant was too deep to disappear and, before long, he was re-admitted to the Theosophical Society. Immediately, he began to foment the idea that the Second Coming, the reappearance of

Christ in physical form, was imminent. He spoke of this figure as a "boddhisattva being," a world teacher, similar to other great teachers. But, of course, he still had to be found.

Not surprisingly, then, at the end of April 1909, Leadbeater found his sought-for "Teacher." He was on the beach at Adyar, India, incarnated in the form of the fourteen year-old boy, Jiddu Krishnamurti (1895-1986). The boy's father, a long-time Theosophist and Assistant Secretary of the Esoteric School in India, happily acquiesced in the identification and willingly gave Leadbeater and Besant permission to adopt the future teacher and his brother. Krishnamurti, known as "Alcyone," soon became the principle focus of theosophical activity. There was no secret about it. In May 1909, at the Budapest Congress, Mrs. Besant spoke to Rudolf Steiner about the new "Teacher," offering Steiner the role of John the Baptist. For Steiner, of course, this was only further and conclusive evidence of the widening split between Adyar and the German Section. For him, as for any Christian, a profound misunderstanding of the nature of the Christ lay behind the claims being made on Krishnamurti's behalf. The Christ could not and would never incarnate physically a second time. The Second Coming was something else. But Steiner's dissent went unheeded.

On January 11, 1911, George Arundale, the principal of the Theosophical Central Hindu College, formed what he called The Order of the Rising Star to prepare for the imminent advent of the new teacher and world savior. Initially, he did not expect his initiative to go much beyond the limits of his college. A few months later, however, Mrs. Besant, deeming many people in various countries ready for such an organization, transformed "The Rising Star" into an international movement and changed its name to "The Order of the Star in the East." The implication was clear. Shortly it would be announced publicly: the new World Teacher was the Savior, Christ. Christ was "reincarnated"!

But, for Rudolf Steiner, this was false. It was nonsense, impossible. In a word, it was anathema. It contradicted the very meaning of the Mystery of Golgotha, theologically and anthroposophically.

(Here it must be stated for the record—and in praise of the Spirit, who always works in mysterious ways—that Krishnamurti when he came of age publicly renounced the high status accorded him and disbanded The Star in the East. Yet he did not fade from the scene, but went on to become one of the most significant spiritual lights of the twentieth century. Leadbeater was thus not in error when he saw something special in the boy; and Krishnamurti, for his part, always—and properly—remained grateful to Theosophy.).

Steiner's response was a threefold deepening of his spiritual research and teaching. The Western tradition needed to be penetrated, understood, and revealed. The truth and reality of the Christ event in its fullness and actuality had to be established. And Anthroposophy—a thoroughly contemporary and free rendering of these—had to be deepened as a way of inner development, a spiritual science, and a way of life.

In 1911, he began to lay down the foundations. He deepened Christology with lecture cycles such as *The Spiritual Guidance of Human Beings and Humanity* (June), *From Jesus to Christ* (October). Individual lectures addressed separate issues, all of which spoke to the true meaning of Christ. There were lectures, for instance, on the life of Christ in relation to the first three years of the child (February and June), as well as various lectures on esoteric Christianity, differentiating the beings of the Buddha, Christian Rosenkreutz, the boddhisattvas, Maitreya Buddha, Jeshu Ben Pandira, and Christ (March, September). At the same time, he focused on the Western tradition with lectures on Goethe, Zoroaster, Galileo and Bruno (January), Hermes / Thoth (February), Greek mythology (August). Anthroposophy—as practice and reality—began to come into its own in such courses as *Occult Physiology* (March), *The Inner Truth of Evolution* (December), *The World of the Senses and the World of the Spirit* (also December), and perhaps above all in the paper he read to the Fourth International Philosophical Congress in Bologna on "The Psychological Foundations and Epistemological Position of Theosophy" (April).

Meanwhile, in the middle of the year, in June, the idea of a "Calendar of the Soul"—quintessential Anthroposophy—was born. It would appear the following Easter in the *Calendar 1912/13*. This *Calendar*, likewise quintessential Anthroposophy, would bear the symbolic motto "In the year 1879 after the birth of the I" and would begin the year with Easter, the feast commemorating the birth of the "I" through the resurrection of Jesus Christ on April 3, 33 of the Common

Era. More esoterically, the *Calendar* would affirm the critical year of 1912 as thirty-three years (that, a repetition of the rhythm of Jesus' earthly life) after 1879, which is the year Rudolf Steiner would come more and more to emphasize that the archangel Michael, under whose aegis Anthroposophy will be placed, celebrated his heavenly victory over the dragon and assumed the regency of the new, evolutionary time period. Clearly, something was about to be born.

On December 10, there was a General Meeting of the German Section. There were now 2,318 members. Six new branches had been founded. There were numerous problems, but none was as decisive as the "Krishnamurti question." Adyar had appointed Dr. Hugo Vollrath, a society member in questionable standing, to be the German representative of the Order of the Star in the East. Dr. Vollrath proclaimed Krishnamurti to be the Christ, and, in the process, attacked Rudolf Steiner. Neither, but especially the former, could be countenanced. A heated debate ensued. Finally, Steiner declared that rather than "expelling" Dr. Vollrath, he should simply "no longer be regarded as a member." Steiner also emphasized that to engage in further argument with Mrs. Besant and her representatives would be useless — he could no longer "defend her"—and proposed that steps be taken to assure the continuity and purity of the spiritual heritage out of which the German Section was working. On December 14, "those who were active on the basis of Rudolf Steiner's work" came together to form an association that, in its statues, had "nothing whatever to do with the Theosophical Society either in form or content."

Against this background, throughout the year 1912, the movement of The Star in the East was gaining strength and membership, and opposition to Rudolf Steiner from Adyar increased. Accusations, harsh words, fantastic assertions (such as Rudolf Steiner was a Jesuit!) began to circulate.

Steiner's program remained largely unchanged. The evolutionary meaning of the Christ event, at once singular and continuing, as well as the more direct articulation of "Anthroposophy" as contemporary spiritual science remained the center of his focus. We may note, above all, *Spiritual Beings in the Heavenly Bodies and in the Kingdoms of Nature* (April); *The Spiritual Foundations of Morality* (May); *The Human*

Being in the Light of Occultism, Theosophy, and Philosophy (June); *The Guardian of the Threshold* and *Initiation, Eternity and the Passing Moment* (August); *According to Mark* (October); *The Bhagavad Gita and the Epistles of Paul* (December.) In September, as if to demonstrate the fundamentally artistic nature of Western, particularly Rosicrucian, esotericism, Rudolf created the new art of eurythmy in response to a request for a "new art of movement." At the same time, prescient of the coming war, Steiner turned increasingly both to research into the meaning of Christ in the twentieth century and the theme of life between death and a new birth. Speaking of the latter, he remarked prophetically:

> Only now is it possible to see the deep moral significance that the supersensible truths relevant to this realm exhibit. Besides all other conditions that make this possible...there is another, at least within our Movement.... This consists in the fact that, if we work intimately and earnestly—really devoting ourselves to and studying this matter—we can enter into what is obtained from the spiritual worlds. It may be said that for a number of years the relation of human beings on the physical plane to the spiritual worlds has changed from what it was, for example, during the whole of the nineteenth century. Until the last third of the nineteenth century, there was little access to the spiritual worlds. In proportion to the necessities of human evolution, very little flowed into human souls out of the spiritual worlds. But now we are living in an age in which a soul needs only to be receptive, needs only to surrender itself and to be prepared, for revelations from the spiritual worlds to pour into it. More and more individual souls are becoming receptive. These are souls for whom, because they are conscious of the mission of their age, the streaming-in of spiritual knowledge is a fact.

1912 thus marked preparation for the true founding of Anthroposophy and the Anthroposophical Society. Throughout the year, the Association formed at the end of 1911 continued to hold meetings. At these, there was much discussion of the importance of karma and reincarnation in building community. In August, Rudolf Steiner proposed that the new Society should be called the "Anthroposophical

Society." Finally, on December 8, the Council of the German Section of the Theosophical Society took the decision that one could no longer be a member in good standing if they also belonged to the Order of the Star in the East. Committed members of The Star in the East were asked to leave the Society. If they did not, they were to be expelled. At the same time, Annie Besant's behavior was considered a betrayal of the fundamental theosophical principle "No knowledge higher than the Truth." Accordingly, on December 11, a telegram was sent, requesting her resignation. The die was cast. On December 28, without further celebration or formality, the "Anthroposophical Society" was founded in Cologne.

1913 was therefore the year in which Rudolf Steiner and Anthroposophy finally shucked the last vestiges of the "Theosophical womb" and stood on their own. On January 2 and 3, the General Meeting for the Founding of the Anthroposophical Society was held. Members and friends from many countries gathered to give a new form to that spiritual community for which Rudolf Steiner had worked the previous eleven years. On January 14, Annie Besant mailed a letter revoking the foundation document of the German Society, thereby formalizing the separation. On February 2 and 3, the matter was concluded with the first, constitutive General Meeting of the Anthroposophical Society.

Rudolf Steiner had held on as long as humanly possible. It had been, as he said, "a martyrdom." Now he had no choice. The intense personal vilification only clarified the complete divergence between what he stood for and what emanated from Adyar. As the meeting opened, he declared openly the fundamental differences: in spiritual orientation, in the conception of the Christ, in esoteric methodology. Mrs. Besant's letter was read. After some discussion, the new Council of the Anthroposophical Society established the definitive break. In conclusion, Rudolf Steiner stated: "The German Section as this has existed from its founding has hereby ended its existence, and all the functions of the German Section have thus come to an end." Many sections and groups from other countries then joined with the Germans and moved their affiliation from Theosophy to Anthroposophy.

Next morning, February 3, Rudolf Steiner opened the General Meeting by saying: "May I call to your attention to the fact that we now stand at the beginning, not of new work, but of a significant endeavor to consolidate and expand.... I hope that we shall find the ways and means to represent more strongly and more devotedly what we fostered in the old form...." He followed these words with a lecture on "The Being of Anthroposophy," which made clear the difference between the old and the new form. *Sophia*—divine feminine wisdom —passing through humanity, becomes *Anthroposophia*:

> People will learn how profoundly what Anthroposophy gives us is based in our whole being. *What we receive through Anthroposophy is our very own being*—which once floated toward us in the form of a celestial goddess with whom we could form a relationship. This divine Being lived on as Sophia and Philosophia. And now we can once again bring her out of ourselves and place her before us as the fruit of true anthroposophical self-knowledge.... It is the essence of Anthroposophy that its own being consists of the being of the human. Its effectiveness and reality consist in that we receive from Anthroposophy what we ourselves are and must place before ourselves because we must practice self- knowledge.

That evening, he opened the first anthroposophical lecture cycle: *The Mysteries of the East and Christianity*. Next day, to set the record straight and respond once and for all to the vilification to which he had been subjected, Steiner spoke briefly on his own life ("Self-Education: Autobiographical Reflections, 1861-1893"). Once that was done, he could set about deepening and expanding the themes that he had broached in preparation for the decisive new beginning represented by the coming into being of the Anthroposophical Society as the true vehicle for his teaching and his mission.

* * *

The stage is now set for the remarkable lectures contained in this volume. Rich and deep, their outer function is to begin to set the record straight after the previous years' chaos, confusion, and misunderstanding of spiritual realities, and thereby to initiate a right orientation to the most momentous task of the moment: to establish a right relationship to Christ and the spiritual worlds, while laying down Anthroposophy as the spiritual path in accord at all levels with the spirit of the times.

Christ and Michael are the explicit guiding lights interwoven in this collection, which itself represents a profound act of Christ-Michael service. Implicitly, too, although mostly unspoken, Sophia—Anthroposophia—is also always present, for it is only in, through, and with her that such service becomes possible in the first place. Thus, with courage, devotion, and conviction, Rudolf Steiner, now free and independent, the "teacher" of his own "school," sets about unveiling the truth and reality as he knows it. The ground has been well laid during the past decade. The esoteric, epistemological, and Christological foundations had been established. All that was necessary was to deepen those foundations and continue building. For Rudolf Steiner, this spirit—under the tutelage of and, indeed, ultimately identical with the archangel Michael, Regent of the Age—is by definition in the service of Christ (whose servant and countenance is Michael). In these lectures, then, Steiner reveals openly, really for the first time, the meaning of such service for him: that Anthroposophists constitute the kernel of a "Michael School" and that he himself and the Anthroposophy that is the fruit and seed of his spiritual research are the earthly representatives of Michael.

The first two lectures were given in London in May. They sound at least four themes, which will echo and deepen throughout the year: 1. "The mission of the Anthroposophical Movement in the spiritual life of the present day;" 2. The primacy of selflessness; 3. The importance of the continuity of the spiritual and physical-sensory worlds; 4. The meaning of the Mystery of Golgotha; and 5. The original, ongoing, and continuing cosmic, historical, and actual presence of Christ and Michael in human evolution both before and after the Mystery of Golgotha.

The volume opens on a universal-human note with wide-ranging discussion of the path of spiritual knowledge or knowing.

Interestingly (in the light of the coming war)—in order to emphasize that inner work has a larger, selfless, cosmic significance beyond our subjective selves— Steiner introduces the idea of a path of knowledge by speaking of "working with dead." He does so by plunging right away into the topic of the spiritual *akashic* substance that surrounds and permeates the world. Whatever human beings achieve in the way of spiritual understanding (or "esoteric science")—what is truly experienced or thought—is inscribed in the akasha. Moreover, only human beings can shape the akasha in this way. Indeed, to do so is one of the chief human tasks—for two reasons. First, when we die, we live in the akasha. Therefore, the akasha is the medium through which the living and the dead can communicate. Those who have not done spiritual work have only memories in the spiritual world, but those who have worked inwardly, experientially, and inscribed the akasha, can continue to "think" and to "think together." This is why contemplative, deep reading—or meditating—in the presence of, or for, the dead can be so fruitful—on both sides of the threshold. But there is more to it. Knowledge of the spiritual worlds can only arise on Earth. The spiritual world can learn about itself only from our work, from what we have inscribed in the akasha. Our work thus has a cosmic significance.

Mostly, of course, we use our faculties, not for spiritual knowing, but for sense- or brain-knowing of the physical world. Such knowledge is thrust aside by the akasha, giving the impression of a conflict in the spiritual world, behind which lie Lucifer and Ahriman. Lucifer first inspired humanity to turn from spiritual truths to knowledge of the physical world, allowing Ahriman to infuse souls with the deadly combination of materialism, egotism, and fear. Anthroposophy, through spiritual science, works to overcome these influences through its inner work of spiritual knowing. As a result of such work, for instance, Rudolf Steiner says, an organ will develop in the brain, which will permit knowledge of previous incarnations. It will render readable what is inscribed in the akasha, i.e., what has been truly, experientially *thought*. For this reason, among others, Anthroposophy, which is a path of knowing that works by enhancing the three principle powers of the soul—thinking, feeling, and willing—must become part of human culture. Intensifying the three soul powers our whole spiritual capacity is transformed, and we become able to assume our full humanity.

The second lecture is one of Rudolf Steiner's most powerful statements on the "renewal of the Mystery of Golgotha in our time," constellating it around two further mysteries: the contemporary role of the archangel Michael in human affairs and the re-appearance of Christ in the etheric as an angel. Underlying his approach is the need to communicate the paradox—itself a mystery—of the unique and incomparable nature both of Christ's death and resurrection *and* his original and ongoing participation in creation and evolution. All of these will be themes—made possible by Anthroposophy's newfound freedom from the shackles of the Krishnamurti affair—that Rudolf Steiner will articulate (and research) through the year.

He begins with Yahweh—as the form of Christ's revelation in the period immediately preceding the Mystery of Golgotha—and his countenance, Michael. Christ-Yahweh, with Michael, "is the being who has accompanied humanity throughout its evolution." Michael, as Yahweh's countenance, guided not only the ancient Hebrews but also the entire previous Michael age: the axial moment of Pythagoras, Plato, Buddha, Aristotle, the Greek tragedians, and so on. This same Michael is now the countenance of Christ and the regent of our age. Michael's teaching is that "the Mystery of Golgotha gives Earth its meaning." On this basis, he will inspire a new "spiritual" science, aided in this by the Mystery event in the spiritual world: "the possibility of perceiving the manifestation of the Etheric Christ—that is to say, Christ in the form of an angel." The dying of Christ consciousness in the sphere of the angels will make possible *direct*, earthly consciousness of Christ.

The following lectures continue and expand the Christ-Michael theme and the presentation of Anthroposophy as the spiritual teaching of the Michael age and, as such, under Michael's aegis. In lecture after lecture, with some repetition but always going deeper, we learn to begin to unravel the intricacies of the complex interrelationship that the Mystery of Golgotha bears to human and cosmic evolution. As the "turning point of time," Christ's incarnation, death and resurrection is, as it were, the unique point that illuminates the whole. For it turns out that the Mystery of Golgotha is the visible heart of an invisible process that encompasses the entirety of what is means to be human.

Rightly understood, the Mystery of Golgotha transforms our understanding not only of history, but also of cosmology and anthropology (which in a sense are one for Rudolf Steiner). As the lectures progress—clearly the result of ongoing, powerful spiritual research—the research into the Mystery of Golgotha deepens until that Mystery becomes, in a real sense, the true key to the great mystery of humanity's place and task in the evolutionary unfolding of the cosmos. The riches here expand with every reading, and it becomes clear that the path of Anthroposophy is an infinite voyage of learning: that reality is truly miraculous.

The earlier lectures focus more on the historical-evolutionary work of Christ. History is illuminated in its unfolding. The present becomes luminous in its significance. Then, toward the end of the volume, Steiner turns to Christ's salvific role in the very formation of human nature. Here, spiritual scientific research produces truly new and revelatory understanding. Although consonant with theology and esotericism, what he discovers has been previously unspoken, because unknown. In these last lectures, Steiner is truly on fire with the experience of insight.

He speaks of Christ's ongoing deeds for humanity's sake—above all, how Christ sacrificed himself three times in the spiritual world *prior* to the great encounter with the Earth, the human "I," and death through the Mystery of Golgotha. We learn how the first sacrifice made it possible for the human sense organs to be selflessly self-clearing, rather than suffering with every sense impression and being unable to get rid of it; how the second sacrifice accomplished a similar deed for the life organs, making it possible for us not to be torn apart by the conflicting desires of our separate organs; and how the third sacrifice made possible the harmony of our human soul forces of thinking, feeling, and willing. As for the Mystery of Golgotha itself, it made possible the right relation of the "I" to the world. Thus—staggering thought—Christ is present in all by which we do—and can—become human. That we can look at the world around us and see its magnificence: for that we must thank Christ. Christ in our senses makes it and our humanity possible. "Not I, but Christ in me" takes on the greatest significance: Christ in our senses, Christ in the health of our organs, Christ in the harmony of our soul functions. Thus we become human—as human beings we are Christ-permeated. As children, we becomes upright, we walk, we speak, we think, we gain the possibility of the selfless "I." Each of the "accomplishments"—without which we would not be human—becomes possible only through Christ's deeds. Truly, we are bound to him in the most intimate ways.

The teaching at the heart of this volume, as it is at the heart of the Christ being himself, is selflessness: the overcoming of egotism and the primacy of the other.

What else than egotism had led to the debacle with Theosophy? What else would lead to the Great War? Where else than egotism is there evil in the world?

As Rudolf Steiner states in the last lecture "What Christ has accomplished for earthly evolution is contained in the fundamental impulse of selflessness. And what he can become for the conscious development of the human soul is the school of selflessness!"

And again: "We must become selfless—that is the task of culture today for the future. Human beings must become more and more selfless. Therein lies the future of right moral life actions, the future of all acts of love that can occur through earthly humanity."

APPROACHING THE MYSTERY OF GOLGOTHA

Rudolf Steiner

1

Esoteric Science and Esoteric Development — Initiation

LONDON, MAY 1, 1913

It is very gratifying for me, visiting this country for the first time,† to greet our English friends here. I regret that I cannot speak to you in your own language, but to overcome this difficulty our friend Baron Walleen will translate what I shall say sentence by sentence; tomorrow, however, I shall deliver the lecture without interruption, and Baron Walleen will be so kind as to give a summary in English.

Our dear friends in this country, who have visited us often on the Continent, have forged an inner bond in the most gracious way between friends here and those on the other side of the Channel. The fine home, where we are gathered today, is proof of the deep inner feeling with which our friends here have united with us to work for the dissemination of Anthroposophy. And those who have traveled from the Continent to greet our English friends will be truly happy to find in this branch so beautiful a frame for what is so dear to our hearts, so deeply rooted in our souls.

Allow me then to speak to you today for the first time and to greet you in the warmest way with that deep, inner feeling of unity that belongs to Anthroposophy, and in which all people on Earth should unite without distinction of race, color, or any such thing. It should be a sound guarantee for our future work that we have found friends who have taken over the work here in this country with such great inner enthusiasm.

Today I want to discuss a topic that takes us directly to a topic that belongs to all humanity, regardless of any differences. I want to speak first about a field of human striving, whose true form cannot be described in any human language, but in its original form only in the language of thoughts: the field of esoteric science.

Human beings strive for occult knowledge and may attain it through their human faculties. But occult knowledge has a greater significance for the world than it has merely within the human soul. In the world around us we can distinguish various substances and materials, through which its various phenomena and manifestations are expressed. All creatures and things of the Earth and of all worlds are rooted in that primal principle which can hardly be expressed in human language. In the physical world, individual instances of this primal principle are expressed in the substances of earth, water, fire, the ether, and so forth.

One of the subtlest substances accessible to human striving is called "akasha."† Beings and phenomena manifested in the akashic substance are the subtlest of all those accessible to human beings. What human beings acquire for themselves in esoteric knowledge not only lives in their souls, but is also impressed in the akashic substance. When we bring an idea from esoteric science to life in our soul, it is immediately inscribed in the akashic substance. It is significant that such impressions, which are significant for the general development of the world, can be inscribed in the akasha only by human beings.

It is important for us to note a special characteristic of the akashic substance. Between death and a new birth, human beings live in that substance, exactly as we, for example, live here within the atmosphere on Earth.

If, with the means at their disposal, seers should come into contact with human souls living between death and new birth, they would observe the following. Human beings who, in the present cycle of earthly development—it was otherwise in earlier times—were never in a position to arouse spiritual-scientific thoughts and ideas in themselves cannot be perceived, even when actually present, by a human soul living between death and a new birth. But if someone living here on Earth has worked with a spiritual-scientific thought or idea, so that it can be inscribed into the akasha, then he or she is perceivable to souls living between death and a new birth. Seers, who have patiently prepared themselves for their gift, can receive deeply moving impressions when they come into contact with souls who have passed through the portals of death. I will give you a perfect example of such a case.

A seer found a man who had gone through the portals of death, leaving behind his wife, whom he deeply loved, and his children, whom he loved no less. This man and his family were likable, good people, but they had no inclination to take spiritual understanding into their souls, and they had never grown beyond the religious traditions through which certain souls even today feel themselves connected with the spiritual world. A while after he had gone through the portals of death, the man came to this realization: I have left behind on Earth my dear wife and children who were the sunshine of my life, but with my spiritual vision I cannot reach them. I have only the memory of the time that I passed with them on Earth.

We see an entirely different picture when a soul that is still on Earth forms clear, strong spiritual thoughts and ideas for itself. In this case, when another soul, living between death and a new birth, looks down on this soul that it has left behind, the soul between death and a new birth can pursue the soul life of the one on Earth in the present because that soul life is inscribing itself into the akashic substance.

Here we touch a point that shows how anthroposophical teaching will remove the chasm between the so-called living and the so-called dead. Today we can already see how people with understanding for the spiritual can be a great blessing for the so-called dead by reading and thinking the truths of spiritual science for them. When we follow in our thoughts, either reading aloud or to ourselves, the ideas and concepts of spiritual science and at the same time feel that one or several of those who have passed through the portals of death are sitting before us while we read, then our reading becomes something very present for them, because such thoughts are inscribed in the akashic substance. And this reading can be of great advantage, not only to those on the other side of death, who studied spiritual science while on Earth, but also to those who wanted nothing to do with it while they were here.

Now, this question could be posed: since the dead are living in the spiritual world, do they really need reading of this sort? Many believe that one has only to go through the portals of death in order to learn everything that can be attained on Earth with the greatest effort through spiritual science. Such people also believe that they need only to die in order to acquire the entire body of esoteric knowledge, because they will then be in the spiritual world. But this is not the case.

Just as here on Earth there are creatures other than human beings (animals, for example) that see everything human beings can see with their senses, but cannot form ideas and concepts about what is seen, so it is with the souls who live in the supersensory world; although they see the beings and facts of the higher spiritual world, they can form no concepts and ideas about them unless people here on Earth inscribe such concepts and ideas in the akashic chronicle.

The mission of human life is thus not insignificant; on the contrary, it is of great significance. If human souls had never lived on Earth, the spiritual worlds would still be there, but no esoteric knowledge of those spiritual worlds would exist. The Earth has reached a point in cosmic evolution where spiritual science can be developed through spiritual beings organized and constituted in the way that human beings are on Earth. What spiritual science inscribes in the akashic substance would never have been there had spiritual science not existed on Earth.

During our present period, people who attempt to examine their soul life on Earth will immediately discover that they have used their activities to acquire knowledge for purposes other than the acquisition of spiritual science. The human faculties for learning are used to acquire knowledge that is called into life by the senses and through intelligence bound to the human brain. Thus, we have human understanding of two kinds: one belongs only to experience acquired through the senses, which requires the organ of intelligence in order to be transformed into understanding; the other is spiritual science. The knowing that belongs only to the sense world forms one stream; the other consists of what people inscribe in the akashic chronicle through spiritual science. Spiritual science works out ideas and concepts that remain eternally written in the akashic chronicle. But when all the knowledge and understanding that belongs to experience gained through the senses—to technical matters, and to the commercial and industrial life of humanity—is inscribed in the akashic substance, the akasha repels this conglomerate of ideas and concepts; in other words, that knowledge and understanding is obliterated.

Anyone who observes the facts I have just mentioned with the eyes of a seer can see a struggle taking place in the akashic substance between impressions made in it by human esoteric science, which are eternal, and those resting on sense data, which are only transient. This struggle arises because, when humankind first began to inhabit the world in the ancient Lemurian epoch,[†] high spiritual beings destined it to acquire spiritual science. But through the intervention of luciferic beings—what we call luciferic influence—humanity directed the power of thinking and the other soul powers it otherwise would have used only for the acquisition of occult ideas and concepts away from them, toward the study of things that belong only to the physical world.

Many people now say that, while ordinary science is open to all, spiritual science can be brought only to those who can see into the spiritual worlds. There is a fundamental fallacy in this statement. In the depths of their souls, all human beings possess, even before they become clairvoyant, the ability and the power to understand the truths of spiritual science. It is true that only the clairvoyant can discover esoteric truths, but once they are discovered and expressed in the normal language of reason, they can be understood by any human soul willing to clear away the impediments to such understanding.

As a result of the luciferic impulses, it became possible later in the development of the Earth for another being, whom we call Ahriman, to gain influence over the souls of human beings. Only when these ahrimanic influences in the soul repressed the possibility of understanding spiritual science did this understanding become unattainable. If the being we call Ahriman were not at work in every human soul, if our souls were without his influence, then an idea or thought of spiritual science would need only to be spoken and a human soul would feel, through its subconscious relationship to this truth in its innermost being, that the idea, the statement of spiritual science, was true.

In every human soul there is not only a life that everyday consciousness understands and can give a reckoning of to itself, but also a subconscious soul life that lies buried as if in the depths of the ocean and is only brought into light from time to time.

The fear of the purely spiritual that is present in every person, for example, belongs to the depths of the soul. This fear is the result of Ahriman's influence and would not exist had Ahriman not gained power over the souls of human beings. People are mostly unconscious of this fear because it works in the deepest foundations of the soul and plays no role in what they can reckon with in their everyday consciousness. Meanwhile, the fear of the spiritual knocks on the door of their ordinary consciousness without their knowing what it is that disquiets them from the depth of their souls. Then they look for something that has an anesthetic effect, something to dull this fear they want no part of. They find the anesthetic in materialistic thoughts, theories, and ideas. Materialistic theories are not invented on logical grounds, although one might believe this to be the case. They are conceived out of a fear of the spiritual, which is the result of Ahriman's influence on the soul.

The preliminary condition for the direct knowledge of spiritual truths is thus much less knowledge of physical science than an education of the soul in the virtue of moral courage, of inner spiritual courage. We may say that, though it is seers who must research esoteric knowledge, it will be understood by all human souls only if those souls are willing to muster all the moral courage they possess in order to eliminate the obstacles originating with Ahriman.

If people desire to understand esoteric truths through the original moral powers of their souls, they can perform the following experiment. They can allow spiritual science to have its effect on their souls without saying beforehand that they agree with this or disagree with that. They can take up spiritual-scientific ideas and concepts given by the seer and allow them to work on their souls. And if they take up esoteric knowledge out of inner enthusiasm rather than mere curiosity, they will experience something that can be compared to a physical floating without ground under their feet, to a feeling as if they were floating in air.

This experiment will have a totally different effect on a person who has religious, reverent inclinations toward spiritual life than it will on someone accustomed to thinking in a materialistic way. A person who has no esoteric knowledge but has inclinations and feelings of a religious nature toward the spiritual world can end up feeling somewhat insecure as a result of this experiment—much less so, however, than a materialist who has no feeling of attraction for the spiritual world. The latter will experience a powerful feeling of fear, of uncertain floating. Materialists can convince themselves with this experiment that occult ideas and concepts touch them in a way that elicits fear and terror. Through an experience of this sort materialists can recognize how full of fear they still are—they are not only fearful of this whole field but fear is one of their fundamental tendencies.

If Ernst Haeckel and Herbert Spencer,† for example, had made this experiment, they would have convinced themselves not only that esoteric knowledge is neither contradictory nor impossible, but also that they were filled with fear from the inmost depths of their souls. Soon they would have forgotten—to a certain extent—all doubt and disbelief about what they usually considered to be the fantasies of spiritual teachings and would have admitted to themselves that it was more important for them to overcome their fear. Once they had made this confession, they would have given up their resistance to what they considered the fantasies of spiritual teachings and understood that they had to try to strengthen in themselves the moral quality of courage. Then they would perhaps have taken their self-education in hand, and if they succeeded in overcoming their fear they would realize that they had become stronger souls and no longer doubted the truth of spiritual science. The experience of strengthening moral courage in the soul is a victory over Ahriman, whose influence can be seen in Haeckel's science and in Spencer's philosophy. Ahriman is the one who inspired souls to take a materialistic path.

Even if only a small part of humanity, as a result of true understanding, works in the way just suggested to strengthen moral courage, all these materialistic theories will gradually disappear from the world.

As we have seen, esoteric knowledge is necessary for the entire process of evolution, because it must be written in the akashic substance. A short sketch of the development of earthly humanity will show us what that means for us. The development of the human race on Earth progresses in steps from one cultural period to the next. During the successive periods human souls inhabit bodies as individualities belonging to these successive cultures of the Earth. All the souls gathered together here this evening were incarnated in bodies belonging to earlier cultural periods. Each individual soul progresses according to the karma it has built for itself.

Beyond this development of individual souls, which depends on their karma, we must recognize the development of the human race as a whole. A Greek body or an Egyptian, Chaldean, ancient Persian, or Atlantean body was in the finer parts of its structure entirely different from a human body of the present age. We must distinguish between the inner progress of the "I" and the astral body from incarnation to incarnation and the external progress and change in the physical and etheric bodies from one race to another, from one nation to another, from one age to another. The progress of the external bodies, the physical and the etheric, from one age to another would not be noticeable to people who study anatomy and physiology, but it is nonetheless present and can be recognized through esoteric science. And the human physical body will be once again totally different in the course of the normal development of humanity when after our present life our souls appear in a future incarnation on Earth.

In the present period of humanity, a delicate organ is being prepared, which is not noticeable to external anatomists and physiologists but exists anatomically. The organ lies in the human brain in the vicinity of the speech center. The development of this organ in the folds of the brain is not the result of the karma of individual souls; rather it is a result of human evolution as a whole on Earth. In the future all human beings will possess this organ, no matter what the development of the souls that incarnate in these bodies may be, and entirely independent from their karma.

Human beings, who are presently inimical to Anthroposophy, as well as those who maintain a sympathetic attitude toward it, will possess this organ in a future incarnation. In the future this organ will be the physical instrument for certain powers of the soul, just as, for example, in the third layer of the brain, Broca's area† is the center for the faculty of speech. When it is developed, humankind can either use it properly or not. It will be used well by those preparing to remember their present life in future incarnations, for this physical organ will be the physical means for recollecting an earlier incarnation.

Today the remembrance of earlier incarnations can be attained only through higher spiritual development, through initiation; but that which in present times can be attained only through initiation will later become in a certain way the common property of the human race. Our present knowledge was earlier the special knowledge of Atlantean initiates. Now everyone can possess it. In the same way, memory of earlier lives on Earth is presently possible only for initiates, but in the future every human soul will possess this capacity.

It is possible for initiates to achieve certain knowledge without the use of a physical organ, but this knowledge can only become the common property of the human race if humanity as a whole in the course of evolution develops an external physical organ through which it can be achieved. Reincarnated souls must nonetheless be able to use this organ correctly to remember earlier incarnations. Only those who have inscribed occult thoughts and ideas clearly in the akashic substance in this present incarnation will be able to use this organ in the proper way.

One often hears people say, "What use is it to believe in earlier lives if people in general are able to remember nothing of them?" One should rather think how much more astonishing it would be if, depending on what one knows of life, human beings in general already could remember their previous lives. If we ask ourselves what is necessary for us to remember anything at all, we must answer that we can only remember what we have previously thought.

Everyday life can teach us this. Think of a person who cannot find his cufflinks when he gets up in the morning. He looks everywhere, but he cannot find them. Why can he not find them? Because he was not thinking about what he was doing while he was putting them away. Let him make an experiment in the opposite sense. Let him, every evening while he puts away his cufflinks, attempt to be fully conscious of himself. "I am putting down my cufflinks in this place." Then he will never lose them, but rather will go directly to the spot where he put them down. Thought will call the action back to his memory.

When we live in a future incarnation, we will remember the past only if we can remember the true nature of the soul, which lives on from one incarnation to the next. Those who have not studied esoteric science in the present life can attain no knowledge of the constitution and nature of the soul, and without this knowledge how could they, when they are incarnated again, remember what they have never thought about in the earlier incarnation?

Through the study of spiritual science, which among other things includes the study of the nature of the soul, we are preparing within us what will make it possible for us to remember in a future life what happened in the present one. Many people today, however, are unwilling to devote themselves to the study of this knowledge. Such people will be reborn, perhaps in their next incarnation, with the aforementioned organ for remembrance of earlier lives physically formed, but they will not have prepared themselves to remember the past.

What sort of significance, then, in the context of what we have said, does spiritual science have in our present life? Through it we attain the possibility of correctly using the organ that will be developed in human beings in the future for remembering earlier earthly lives. In our present incarnation we must inscribe the knowledge of our soul in the akashic substance in order to use this organ, which is developing in human beings, whether they wish it or not, for remembering earlier lives in the right way. In the future there will be people who can use the organ for remembering earlier lives on Earth and others who will not be able to use it. Certain diseases will manifest in the latter, because they will have an organ in their physical body they cannot use. Possessing an organ and being unable to use it calls forth nervous diseases of a very particular kind, and these nervous ailments will be far worse than all that human beings have known until now.

If one observes in this way the interrelationship of the facts, one begins to get an idea of the mission of spiritual science and of the true significance of an understanding of life and of the human being through the study of this knowledge. In case the impression this observation has made on you might lead to misunderstandings, let me mention yet another fact, which can alleviate whatever in this impression might have made you feel uncomfortable. Although the true esotericist can see that spiritual science must enter the spiritual life of our present time so that people in the future can use the organ for remembrance and remain in good physical health, at the same time it cannot be maintained that those who in the present time are not ready to take up spiritual science will be lost in their following incarnation in the manner previously described. For a long time into the future, it will still be possible for people, even if they have neglected what I said—and have not used the organ for remembrance in this particular life—to make it up in the following life. They will still have some opportunities to restore their health and to attain spiritual-scientific truths. But the time will come when this will no longer be possible.

Even if we have not yet reached that particular moment, we still live in the period of humanity when, for the reasons already mentioned, spiritual science must be integrated into the spiritual life of humanity. It is a necessary development in the general progress of humanity and does not originate from the personal opinions of one or the other individual. Moreover, in this way and especially in this time, the possibility for the subjective development of the human soul will be granted, which will lead to a personal vision of the spiritual worlds, to esoteric development. We can say that all persons who use the pure, original powers within their souls, untroubled by ahrimanic influences, can understand everything that is revealed in our spiritual worlds, and it is in a certain sense possible for all human beings to raise themselves into the spiritual worlds through the spiritual development they have undergone. In the present, three forces of the soul can be developed well enough so that an esoteric connection with the supersensory worlds can take place.

The first force that can be developed in the human soul is the force of *thinking*. We live in the context of the world that surrounds us because of the thoughts we form about our environment. In ordinary, everyday life, people think thoughts caused either by sense impressions or through the intellect, which is bound to the brain. In my book *How to Know Higher Worlds*,† you will find how a person, through meditation, concentration, and contemplation, through the strengthening of the soul life, can make this force of thinking independent from external life.

At this point, in particular, I want to make you aware of how one can make the power of thinking—which otherwise is developed only through one's activity of forming thoughts about the external world—free and independent from everything that belongs to the body. This means that through such a development the soul attains the ability to think, to form thoughts, without making use of the body, without using the brain as a tool. We can understand this well if we look at the chief characteristic of ordinary, everyday thinking, which is dependent upon impressions gained through the senses.

The main characteristic of ordinary thinking is that every individual action of thinking takes its toll on the nervous system, especially the brain; it destroys something in the brain. Each everyday thought means a destructive process, in miniature, in the brain cells. Hence we need sleep so that this process of destruction can be repaired. During sleep, we replace what has been destroyed during the day through thinking. What we perceive in an ordinary thought is in reality a process of destruction that takes place in our nervous system.

Let us now attempt to develop a meditation that we give ourselves over to, for example, in the contemplation of the following:

Wisdom lives in the light.

This idea cannot derive from sense impressions because, for the external senses, it is not true that wisdom lives in the light. In such a situation we restrain the thinking through meditation so that it does not connect itself to the brain. If in this way we develop an inner activity of thinking that is not connected to the brain, we will feel, through the effects of such a meditation on our soul, that we are on the right path. Since in meditative thinking we do not call forth any destructive process, thinking of this sort will never make us sleepy, no matter how long it is carried on, something that our ordinary thinking can easily do.

It is true that often the very opposite transpires when one meditates, for people often complain that when they give themselves to meditation they fall asleep instantly. It is perfectly natural that in meditation we first use the kind of thinking to which we have otherwise always been accustomed. Only with time do we become accustomed to ceasing outer thinking. When we reach this point, meditative thinking no longer makes us sleepy, and this is how we will know that we are on the right track.

When we develop the inner power of thinking in this way, without the thinking force of the external body, we will attain knowledge of our inner life; we will know our true self, our higher "I."

One can find the way to true knowledge of the human self in the kind of meditation just described, which leads to the liberation of inner thinking. Only through such knowledge can one reach the point of seeing that the human self is not bound within the limits of the physical body. On the contrary, one learns to understand that this self is connected with the phenomena of the world around us. While in ordinary life we see the Sun here, the Moon there, there the mountains, hills, plants, and animals, we now feel ourselves connected with everything we see and hear; we are only a part of it. For us there is then only one external world, and that is our body. While in ordinary life we are here, and the external world is around us, after the development of the power of independent thinking we are outside our bodies, at one with what we otherwise see; while our body, which we are otherwise within, is outside ourselves. We look back at it; it has become the only world we can see from without.

In this way, through the liberation of one's power of thinking, we can truly step outside our physical body and observe it as something external. We can do even more. We can, for example, give a positive answer to the question "Why do we wake up every morning?" During sleep our physical body lies in bed, and we are in fact outside of it, just as is the case during meditative thinking. In awakening we return to the physical body, because like a magnet hundreds and thousands forces draw us back to it. People commonly know nothing of this, but when they free themselves through meditation, they are consciously drawn back through the same force that in the previous instance draws the soul unconsciously back into the physical body on awakening.

We learn through a meditation of this sort how human beings descend from the higher worlds in which they have lived between death and a new birth, and how they connect themselves with the forces and substances given to them through parents, grandparents, and so forth. In short, we learn to recognize the forces that, between death and a new birth, draw people back into a new incarnation.

As the result of such a meditation, one can look back on a great part of the life that was passed before birth, before conception, in the spiritual world between death and a new life. However, through the meditation just described, one mostly can only look back to a certain point situated before the last incarnation; one cannot look back further into earlier incarnations. At present, as long as the previously mentioned organ has not yet been formed in the human brain, another form of meditation other than the thought meditation just described is necessary in order to look back into earlier incarnations. This other meditation can take place only if *feeling* is brought into the object of meditation. Everything just described as meditation can be infused with feeling.

Let us now consider the content of meditation that, in the meditation itself, must be infused with feeling and sensitivity. For example, let us take as content:

Wisdom shines forth in the light.

If we feel ourselves inspired by the radiance of wisdom, if we feel ourselves exalted, if we are illuminated within by this content, if we live within it with enthusiastic feelings and are able to meditate on it, then we have something more before our soul than meditation in thought. The power and the force of feeling that we use in the soul are what we otherwise use in speech. Speech is brought forth when we thoroughly infuse our thoughts with inner feeling, with inner sensitivity. This infusion with feeling is the origin of speech, and Broca's area in the brain is brought into play in this manner: the thoughts of inner life that are shot through with inner sensitivity become active in the brain and form the organ that is the physical instrument of speech.

If we meditate thus, if our meditation is truly infused with such feelings, then we hold back in our souls the force that we use for speech in daily life. We can say that speech, if it is the embodiment of the inner power of the soul, expresses these thoughts interpenetrated with feeling. If instead of allowing the soul force to emerge in speech we develop meditation from these feeling-infused thoughts, if we go further and further with this meditation, then we will gradually develop the ability, even without the physical organ, to look backward by means of initiation into earlier lives on Earth and also into the time between the earthly lives, the time that always lies between death and a new life.

Through this kind of training in the retention of speech within the soul, or, as esotericists say, through the retention of the Word within the soul, we can look back to the very beginning of our Earth, back to what the Bible calls the creative act of the elohim. We can look backward as far as the time when repeated earthly lives began for the human race, for the esoteric development we reach through restraining the Word, or speech, enables us to look into successive periods of time insofar as they are connected with our Earth, with the spiritual life of Earth. However, these two forces of clairvoyance developed through thoughts and thoughts infused with feeling cannot lead us to experiences that lie before the time of the Earth that exists today, to experiences linked to earlier planetary incarnations of our Earth. To experience those, a third meditative force is necessary, which we now wish to speak about briefly.

We can infuse the content of our meditation with the impulses of *the will* in such a way that, when we meditate, for example on "The wisdom of the world shines forth in the light," we can truly feel, without willing it externally, the impulse of our will yoked to that activity. We can feel our own being connected to the radiant force of light and can make this light shine and vibrate through the world. We must feel the impulse of our will yoked to this meditation.

When we meditate in such a way that our meditation is filled with the impulse of the will, we restrain a force that otherwise would flow into the pulsation of the blood. You can easily observe that the life of our inner "I" can flow into the pulsing of the blood if you recall that we become pale when we are afraid and blush when we are ashamed. That is the overflow of soul force into the pulsation of the blood. When this same force that influences the blood enters activity in such a way that it does not descend into the physical, but remains in the soul alone, this third meditation begins, which we can influence through impulses of the will.

If those who work through these three forms of esoteric development only liberate their force of thinking, they feel as if they have an organ at the root of the nose. This organ is described as the lotus flower, through which one can take note of the "I," or self, that is stretched far out into space. Those who develop feeling-infused thoughts through meditation will eventually become conscious through this developed force, which otherwise would become speech, of the so-called sixteen-petalled lotus flower in the area of the Adam's apple. With the assistance of this lotus flower one can comprehend everything associated with time-bound things from the beginning of Earth to its end. Through this organ one learns also to understand the esoteric significance of the Mystery of Golgotha, which we shall speak about in our next lecture. Through the restrained soul force that in normal daily life would extend into the blood and its pulsation, an organ in the region of the heart is developed (described in my book *An Outline of Esoteric Science*) through which one can understand the evolution of the earlier incarnations of our Earth, described in esoteric circles as Saturn, Sun, and Moon.

You see, then, that no assertion is being made that esoteric development is gained through anything that is impossible or nonexistent, but rather through what is really available within the human soul. The first esoteric power that was mentioned originates from a higher development of the force of thinking, the power that is otherwise used only for thoughts connected with the external world. The second power we have spoken about is only a higher development of what is applied externally by every human being through the body in speech in the development of the organ for the Word. The third power is a higher formation of what is otherwise present in the human soul to cause the blood to pulse faster or slower, to lead a smaller or larger quantity of blood to this or that organ in the body—more to the middle when we are pale, more to the surface when we blush, more or less to the brain, and so forth.

When human beings train these powers, which are available to them but in ordinary life are used only for their external physical existence, then esoteric development begins. And what can be known through esoteric development can be understood and comprehended by any person willing to clear out the obstacles to understanding. What can be learned through esoteric development is esoteric science, and in our present cycle of humanity esoteric science must flow into the human soul so that this soul can learn to know its own nature, which is independent of the body. The forms of all of the substances in the external world, like earth, water, air, and so forth, pass away; the forms of the akashic substance live on. Our soul must feel itself yoked with the akashic substance through its inner life, and in future times it will have the desire to remember what it has experienced in the present. The possibility to attain ideas and concepts that can lead to such a memory is the result of the study of spiritual science, which is only possible when esoteric knowledge is disseminated and accepted.

I have therefore attempted to make clear to you in this first lecture how absolutely necessary the dissemination of occult knowledge is, as well as directions for occult development and the impulses at the foundation of the development of humanity. I have not used words based on ordinary human observations to try to elucidate the mission of esoteric science, but rather the observation of facts that are the fruit of esoteric research. Those who allow these facts to work on their souls will grasp that it is impossible for anyone who understands the full importance of these facts to deny the necessity of the dissemination of spiritual-scientific knowledge in the present day. One does not have to become a fanatic to recognize the necessity for the corresponding training; one needs only to understand the facts that lie at the foundation of the esoteric life of humanity.

Furthermore, we can say that only ignorance of these facts can keep humanity away from the anthroposophical life. Therefore spiritual science, as it is understood here, will be the least fanatical among the spiritual movements of our time, as well as the one that emerges most from objective observations. It is especially necessary to mention over and over again that all such theories, all such doctrines, must finally come together within the purview of Anthroposophy as a fundamental lively feeling.

There is an objective spiritual life, whose reflection in the world of maya is the life that surrounds us. Esoteric development is to withdraw from the world of maya and to penetrate with the best powers of our "I" into the world of spiritual reality. Each step we make in esoteric knowledge and in esoteric development is a step from appearance to reality. And because a true understanding of this fact can lead to no other impulse than to realize these steps, the fate of spiritual science is assured, because more and more souls will desire to recognize the truth about the spirit of the cosmos. The anthroposophical fire that can be kindled in us is only a result of the universal cosmic fire, which flows forth from the beginning to the end.

This is what I wanted to tell you in this first lecture on the mission of the Anthroposophical Movement in the spiritual life of today.

2

Christ at the Time of the Mystery of Golgotha and Christ in the Twentieth Century

LONDON, MAY 2, 1913

THE Mystery of Golgotha is the most difficult of all mysteries to understand, even for those already advanced in spiritual knowledge, and is the most easily misunderstood of all truths to which human beings can relate. This mystery was a powerful impulse in the development of humanity on Earth. It was a unique event in the evolution of the Earth, one that had never happened before in the same way and will never happen again in the same manner. Human understanding is always looking for a standard, for a comparison in relation to which things can be understood, but something that is incomparable cannot be compared. Because it is unique, it is understood only with difficulty.

We have tried in the spiritual-scientific movement to characterize this Mystery of Golgotha from different perspectives. New points of view can constantly be chosen and new characteristics continually brought forth to describe this mighty event in the evolution of humanity. A new perspective of this sort will be presented here today. In particular, attention will be drawn to what can be called in a certain sense the renewal of the Mystery of Golgotha in our time, in our present cycle of humanity.

If we want to understand the Mystery of Golgotha in depth, we should not regard it as something entirely separated from the whole evolution of humanity, as an object of consideration only for its duration of three or thirty-three years. Rather, we should consider why and how it came to pass precisely in the fourth post-Atlantean age, the so-called Greco-Roman cultural period. We should also take into consideration that it was prepared during the entire development of the ancient Hebrew people. What took place in the human sphere in the fourth post-Atlantean age is highly important for the Mystery of Golgotha, and also of considerable importance is what was prepared over the entire course of ancient Hebrew culture—the veneration of Yahweh. First, it is important to understand who the being was that revealed himself in the times of the ancient Hebrews under the name of Yahweh.

Human beings today are, above all, beings who develop their intellect in the context of what affects their reason and their capacity of understanding—what develops their intellect. They love to understand things from an intellectual point of view. However, the moment one crosses the threshold from the world of the senses to the supersensible world, the possibility of understanding reality exclusively with intellectual means ends. Human understanding can render good service on Earth, but the moment one enters the supersensible world it is no longer sufficient as a means of acquiring knowledge, although it can still be a useful tool.

Human understanding is above all fond of making distinctions. To understand something requires a definition. Those among you who have attended my lectures relatively often will have noticed the lack of almost any kind of definition. One cannot comprehend the objects of reality through definitions. There are, to be sure, good definitions and bad definitions, definitions that are comprehensive and others that are less satisfactory. Definitions are necessary to understand earthly matters, but if one wishes to understand things that pertain to reality, namely things that pertain to the supersensible reality, then one cannot make definitions. One must describe—characterize, depict—for it is necessary to consider facts and entities from all points of view.

Definitions are always one-sided and remind a person who has studied such things of the logic of the ancient Greek philosophical school that once sought to define what a human being is. To give an idea of a human being, the following definition was proposed: "A human is a two-legged creature without feathers." The next day someone brought in a plucked rooster and said, "This is a two-legged creature without feathers; consequently it is a human being." One can often be reminded of this when definitions are demanded for something so many-sided and polyvalent that definitions are insufficient and one can only describe it. However, in order to be able to distinguish the different entities in the supersensible world, people find a definition desirable. They ask, "Exactly what is such an entity?" The further one penetrates into the supersensible worlds, the more the entities there interpenetrate one another. There is no longer any boundary between them, so it is difficult to distinguish one from the other.

Above all, we may not ignore the factor of evolution when considering the name Yahweh, especially when we relate it to the name of Christ. Even in the New Testament you will find (and I have often referred to this in my books) that Christ revealed himself through Yahweh, as far as he could, before the Mystery of Golgotha.

If one wishes to compare Yahweh with Christ, it is a good idea to use the image of sunlight and moonlight. What is sunlight? What is moonlight? They are one and the same, yet very different. Sunlight radiates from the Sun, but in moonlight sunlight is thrown back from the Moon. In the same way, Christ and Yahweh are one and the same. Christ is like the sunlight, and Yahweh is like the reflected Christ light, insofar as this light could reveal itself to the Earth under the name Yahweh before the Mystery of Golgotha intervened. Moreover, when such an exalted being as Yahweh-Christ comes into question, we must look into the lofty heights of the supersensible worlds for the true meaning. In reality it is presumptuous to approach such an entity as Yahweh-Christ with everyday concepts.

The ancient Hebrews tried to find a way out of these difficulties. The human power of thinking is weak, but they attempted to form an idea of this exalted being. Attention was not directed directly at Yahweh (a name essentially regarded as not to be spoken), but rather at the being described in western literature as Michael. Much misunderstanding can arise from this assertion, but that is unavoidable. One person could perhaps say that this might reawaken Christian prejudices; another wants nothing to do with such things. But the being we may call Michael who belongs to the hierarchy of the archangels (however we might wish to call this being) nonetheless exists. And there are many beings of this sort who belong to the same rank. However, this particular being, who is known esoterically as Michael, is as exalted among his companions as the Sun is with respect to the planets—Venus, Mercury, Jupiter, Saturn, and so forth.

Michael is the most excellent and significant being in the hierarchy of the archangels. The ancients called Michael "God's face." Just as people reveal themselves through their gestures and facial expressions, so was Yahweh understood in ancient mythology through Michael. Yahweh made himself recognizable to initiates in such a manner that they were able to grasp something that previously their normal capacity of understanding would never have been able to understand, specifically, that Michael is the face of Yahweh. Hence the ancient Hebrews spoke of Yahweh-Michael as Yahweh, the unapproachable, whom one could never reach, just as one cannot reach the thoughts, sufferings, and cares that lie behind other human beings' public faces. Michael is the external manifestation of Yahweh, just as the manifestation of other human beings is recognized in their brows and faces.

So we can say that Yahweh manifested himself through Michael, one of the archangels. The recognition of what we have described as Yahweh was not limited to the Hebrews. It was far more widespread, and if we investigate the five centuries before the Christian era we find that during this whole time a revelation took place through Michael. We could discover this revelation in another form in Greek philosophy, in Plato, Socrates, or Aristotle, even in the ancient Greek tragedies during the five centuries before the Golgotha event.

If we try to illuminate with the help of occult knowledge what really happened, we can say that Christ-Yahweh is the being who has accompanied humankind throughout its entire evolution. However, during the successive epochs, Christ-Yahweh always revealed himself through different beings of the same rank as Michael. He chooses to speak constantly with a different face, to turn a different face toward humanity. And depending on which one from the hierarchy of the archangels is chosen to be the mediator between Christ-Yahweh and humanity, very different ideas and constructs, impulses of feeling, impulses of will, and so forth, are manifested. We can describe the whole period surrounding the Mystery of Golgotha as the age of Michael, and we can consider Michael to be the emissary of Yahweh.

In the period that preceded the Mystery of Golgotha for approximately five hundred years and continued on for several centuries after it, the leading culture of humanity bore the stamp of Michael, so to speak. Through his characteristics, his power, everything that should have been bestowed on humanity at that time flowed into it. And then other beings came, other beings from the order of the archangels, who were likewise inspirers of humankind from the spiritual worlds.

As was just mentioned, Michael was the greatest archangel, the most powerful, the most important, so an epoch like Michael's is always the most significant, or one of the most significant, that can occur in the development of humanity. The epochs of the different archangels repeat themselves, and it is a fact of greatest importance that each being from the archangelic hierarchy gives an age its fundamental character. Archangels are primarily the leaders of the different nations, but because they become the leaders of different epochs and because they are also the leaders of bygone ages, they are in a certain sense also the leaders of all humanity.

As regards Michael, a change occurred just before our present evolutionary cycle. Michael underwent a process of development. This is of the greatest importance. According to esoteric knowledge, a couple of decades ago [1879], we once again entered an epoch inspired by the same being who inspired the age in which the Mystery of Golgotha took place. Since the end of the nineteenth century we may look at Michael as our leader.

If we wish to understand this, we must consider the Mystery of Golgotha from another point of view and ask ourselves, what is the primary significance in this mystery? What is of utmost significance is that the being, who is distinguished by the name Christ, went through the Mystery of Golgotha and through the portals of death at that time. Never in the whole of earthly evolution could one speak of the Mystery of Golgotha without considering as the most important aspect of this mystery the fact that Christ went through death.

Consider the laws of nature. Much may be understood by studying them, and in the future evolution of the Earth much more still may be learned, but we are mere dreamers if we do not recognize that the understanding of life as such is an ideal that can be understood only through inner development and never through the study of the laws of nature. There are indeed dreamers in our day who believe that true understanding of the principle of life will be attained in the fullness of time through scientific knowledge; but that will never be the case. During the course of earthly evolution many laws are yet to be discovered through the senses, but the principle of life as such can never reveal itself in this way. Such a revelation can occur only through the methods of esoteric knowledge.

Therefore life appears to us as something that on Earth is inaccessible to science. And just as life is inaccessible to human knowledge, so is it the case with death in relation to true knowledge, attained in the supersensible worlds. In the entire realm of the supersensible worlds, there is no death. One can only die on Earth, in the physical worlds or in worlds developmentally equivalent to our world, and all the beings in the hierarchies of higher rank than the human have no knowledge of death. They know only different states of consciousness. Their consciousness can from time to time sink so far that it resembles our earthly state of sleeping, but they can awaken again from this sleep. There is no death in the spiritual world; there is only transformation of consciousness. One who has risen after death into the supersensible worlds cannot experience the greatest fear a human being has, the fear of death. The moment human beings go through the portals of death, their condition is of such an intense sensitivity that, although they can exist in a darkened state of consciousness, it would be very odd indeed to imagine that a person in the supersensible world was dead.

Hence there is no death for the beings who belong to the higher hierarchies, with only one exception—Christ. However, for a supersensible being like Christ to go through death, he must first descend to Earth. And this is what is of such immeasurable importance in the Mystery of Golgotha: that a being, who in his realm, in the sphere of his will, would never have been able to experience death, was obliged to descend to Earth in order to work through the experience of death. Through the fact that this being underwent death in order to share this fate with humanity, a deep inner bond was established between humankind on

Earth and Christ. This death, as I have just emphasized, is of the greatest significance, above all for our present earthly evolution.

What really happened back then in respect to our evolution on Earth has already been discussed often. First of all, a unique being, who until then had existed only on a cosmic level, united himself with earthly evolution through the Mystery of Golgotha, through Christ's death. He entered the evolution of the Earth at the time of the Mystery of Golgotha. He wasn't there before. He belonged to the cosmos, but through the Mystery of Golgotha, he came down from the cosmos and took bodily form on Earth. Since then he lives in such a way on Earth, is so much bound to the Earth, that he lives in the souls of human beings on Earth and experiences life on Earth together with them. Hence the whole period before the Mystery of Golgotha was only a time of preparation in the evolution of Earth. The Mystery of Golgotha gave the Earth its meaning.

When the Mystery of Golgotha took place, the earthly body of Jesus of Nazareth (as we know from the various reports we possess) was given over to the elements of Earth, and from that time on, Christ was bound up with the spiritual sphere of Earth and lives within it. It is, as we have already said, exceptionally difficult to describe the Mystery of Golgotha, since we have no standard with which to compare it, but still we want to attempt to approach it from yet another point of view.

Christ lived, as we know, for three years after the baptism in the Jordan in the body of Jesus of Nazareth as a human being among the people of the Earth.† We can call this the earthly manifestation of Christ in a physical human body. How then does the Christ being manifest, since he laid aside his physical body in the Mystery of Golgotha?

We must of course picture the Christ being as an overwhelmingly high being, but although so exalted, he was nevertheless able to bring himself to expression in a human body for the three years following the baptism by John in the Jordan. But how does he reveal himself since then? Certainly, he no longer reveals himself in the human body, since that was given over to the Earth and now forms a part of it. To those who have, through the study of esoteric science, developed within themselves the possibility of looking into these matters, it will be revealed that this being can now be recognized in one of the beings belonging to the hierarchy of the angels. Just as the Redeemer of the World, this Christ being, although of such an exceptional loftiness, manifested himself in a human body during the three years following the baptism in the Jordan, so has he manifested himself since that time in a direct way as an angelic being, a spiritual being standing one step higher than humanity. As such, clairvoyants could always find him; as such, he was always bound to evolution. As true as it was that Christ, while incarnated in the body of Jesus of Nazareth, was more than a human being, so is the Christ being more than an angel. That is only his external form. However, in the fact that a powerful, lofty being descended, as we have described, from the spiritual worlds and dwelt for three years in a human body, the further fact is also brought to expression: during this time, this being progressed one step further in his own development.

When such a being accomplishes such a deed while assuming a human or angelic form, he himself progresses. And that is what we have alluded to in the development of Christ-Yahweh. Christ has reached the condition in which he will manifest himself from now on, not as a human being, not only through his reflected light, not only through the name of Yahweh, but directly. Here is the great difference in all the teachings and wisdom that have entered the earthly evolution since the Mystery of Golgotha—through the arrival of the Michael spirit on Earth, through his inspiration, humankind could now gradually begin to understand everything that the Christ impulse, the Mystery of Golgotha, means. Earlier, Michael was the emissary of Yahweh, who is the reflection of Christ's light; he was not yet the emissary of the Christ being itself.

Michael inspired humanity through several centuries, for approximately five hundred years before the Mystery of Golgotha, as indicated in the ancient mysteries and by Plato. However, soon after the Mystery of Golgotha took place and the Christ being united himself with the evolution of Earth, the direct influence of Michael came to an end. At the time that those ancient documents we have in the form of the Gospels were written (as I have described in my *Christianity as Mystical Fact*), Michael himself lost the ability to inspire humanity; but through his companions among the archangels, humanity was inspired in such a way that much soul force was acquired unconsciously through inspiration.

The evangelists themselves had no clear esoteric knowledge, because the inspiration of Michael came to an end shortly after the event of the Mystery of Golgotha. The other archangels, the companions of Michael, could not inspire humanity in a way that would make the Mystery of Golgotha understandable, which explains the contradictory interpretations of the different Christian teachings. The companions of Michael inspired much in these teachings, but they Michael himself did not inspire them. Rather they stand in relation to his inspiration as the planets stand to the mighty Sun.

Now, in our time, another such influence is present, a direct inspiration from Michael. This direct inspiration from Michael has been prepared since the sixteenth century. During that period, the archangels who stood closest to Michael gave humanity the inspiration that led to the fulfillment of natural science in our modern time. The natural science of the present day does not come from the inspiration of Michael, but from one of his companions, Gabriel. This scientific inspiration tends to create a body of knowledge, a point of view that provides understanding of the material world alone and exists overall in relation to the physical brain.

Within the last couple of decades, Michael† has again taken over the place of this inspirer of science, and in the next couple of centuries Michael will give the world something just as important in the spiritual sense—indeed, even more important, immeasurably more important, because it is more spiritual—as material science that since the sixteenth century has progressed from level to level. Just as his archangelic companion once gave the world science, so will Michael give us spiritual knowledge in the future. We find ourselves at the beginning of this. Just as Michael was sent five hundred years before the Mystery of Golgotha as the emissary of Yahweh, the reflection of Christ, to give that era its own stamp, just as he was the emissary of Yahweh then, so has Michael become the emissary of Christ for our time. Just as in ancient Israelite times, which were a direct preparation for the Mystery of Golgotha, ancient Hebrew initiates could turn to Michael as the external manifestation of Yahweh, so we are now in a position to turn to Michael, who has evolved from the emissary of Yahweh into the emissary of Christ, to receive increasing spiritual revelation over the next two centuries that will unveil the Mystery of Golgotha more and more. That which took place two thousand years ago—which could be communicated only through the various Christian sects and whose depths can be laid bare only in the twentieth century when instead of science, spiritual knowledge, the gift of Michael, will come into action—will fill our hearts with immeasurably deep feelings for the spiritual in our time. We will be able to realize that in the past two decades a gate has opened through which understanding can enter.

Michael can give us new spiritual light, which we may regard as a transformation of the light given through him at the time of the Mystery of Golgotha, and people of today may stand in this light. If we can experience this, we can grasp the full meaning of the new age that is emerging just now from our own. We can take note of the dawning of a spiritual revelation, which will enter the life of human beings on Earth in the next two centuries. In fact, since humanity is freer than it was before, we will be able through our own will to advance to the point of being able to receive this revelation.

Let me now indicate the event in the higher worlds that has led to this altered situation, this time of a renewal of the Mystery of Golgotha. Looking back, let us recall what has probably often flowed through our souls—namely, what happened at the baptism by John in the Jordan when the Christ manifested himself in human form visible to human beings on Earth. Further, we let us fill our souls with the thought of that occasion when the Christ, as far as outer form was concerned, united himself with the hierarchy of the angels to live since then invisibly on Earth.

Let us remember what has been said, that death does not exist in the invisible worlds. Christ, by descending to our world, passed through a death similar to that of human beings. Since he became again a purely spiritual being, he has always kept the memory of his death with him. As a being from the rank of the angels, however, among whom since then he has continued to manifest himself outwardly, he could experience only a diminution of consciousness.

By means of what has been necessary since the sixteenth century for the Earth's evolution—specifically the ever-increasing triumph of science—something that is also significant for the invisible worlds has intervened in the whole evolution of humanity. With the triumph of science, materialistic and agnostic feelings (of greater intensity than had previously been the case) penetrated humanity. Materialistic tendencies had existed even earlier, but never of the intensity that became predominant in the sixteenth century. More and more, when human beings entered the spiritual worlds through the portals of death, they brought with them the result of their materialistic ideas on Earth, so that after the sixteenth century more and more seeds of earthly materialism were constantly carried over. These seeds developed in a particular way.

Although Christ entered the ancient Hebrew race and was led to his death there, the angelic being who has been the external form of Christ has suffered a dissolution of consciousness in the course of the nineteen century as a result of the opposing materialistic forces that rose into the spiritual worlds consequent upon materialistic human souls passing through the portals of death. And the emergence of unconsciousness in the spiritual worlds as the result of materialism in the manner just described will lead to the resurrection of Christ consciousness in the twentieth century in the souls of human beings on Earth between birth and death.

In a certain sense, one can predict from this that, from the twentieth century onward, what humanity has lost in consciousness will certainly arise again for clairvoyant perception. In the beginning only a few, then a constantly increasing number of beings in the twentieth century will be capable of perceiving the appearance of the etheric Christ, that is, Christ in the form of an angel. For the sake of humanity, something that can be called a destruction of consciousness occurred in the worlds lying directly above our earthly worlds, in which Christ has been visible between the Mystery of Golgotha and the present day.

One can say that, at the time of the Mystery of Golgotha, something happened in a little known corner of Palestine that was in fact the greatest event that ever happened to all of humanity, but of which little notice was taken by people of the time. If something like that can happen, can we be surprised when we hear what happened in the nineteenth century when those who had passed through the portals of death since the sixteenth century encountered Christ?

"The seeds of earthly materialism"—which souls stepping through the portals of death since the sixteenth century have carried up to the spiritual world in ever-greater proportion, creating more and more darkness—make up the "black sphere of materialism." This black sphere was taken up by the Christ into his being in the sense of the Manichaean principle,† effecting a "spiritual death by suffocation" in the angelic host among whom the Christ being has manifested himself since the Mystery of Golgotha. This sacrifice of Christ in the nineteenth century is comparable to the sacrifice on the physical level in the Mystery of Golgotha and can be designated as the second crucifixion of Christ on the etheric level. The spiritual death by suffocation that accompanied the dissolution of consciousness of the angelic being is a repetition of the Mystery of Golgotha in the worlds lying directly behind ours, so that a resurrection of the previously hidden Christ consciousness can take place in the souls of human beings on Earth. This return to life is in the process of becoming the clairvoyant vision of humanity in the twentieth century.

Christ consciousness can thus be united with the earthly consciousness of humanity from the twentieth century on, because the dying out of Christ consciousness in the angelic sphere in the nineteenth century means the resurrection of direct Christ consciousness in the sphere of the Earth. That is, the life of Christ will, from the twentieth century on, be felt increasingly in the souls of human beings as a direct personal experience.

At the time of Christ, a few people existed who could read the signs of the time and were able to understand the Mystery of Golgotha. They could grasp how a great and powerful being had descended from the spiritual worlds to live on Earth, passing through death, so that, through his death, his being's substances could be incorporated into the Earth. Similarly today, some of us can perceive that in certain worlds lying directly behind ours, a kind of spiritual death, a dissolution of consciousness, took place so that a rebirth of the earlier hidden Christ consciousness could take place in the souls of human beings on Earth.

Since the Mystery of Golgotha took place, many people can proclaim the name of Christ, and from the twentieth century on there will be a constantly increasing number of people who can communicate the knowledge of the Christ being given in spiritual science. Twice already Christ has been crucified: the first time physically in the physical world at the beginning of our era, and a second time in the nineteenth century spiritually, I have described. One could say that humanity experienced the resurrection of the Christ being's body then; from the twentieth century on, it will experience the resurrection of Christ consciousness.

What I have only been able to suggest in a few words will gradually penetrate human souls, and the mediator, the emissary, will be Michael, who is now the emissary of Christ. Just as he led human souls in earlier times so that they could understand the movement of the Christ being's life from heaven to Earth, so is he now preparing humanity to become capable of experiencing the movement from the state of unconsciousness to the state of consciousness. And exactly as most people at the time of Christ's life on Earth were incapable of believing what a mighty event took place in the evolution of the Earth, the external world in our time is striving to increase the power of materialism, and will continue for a long time to regard what we have discussed today as fantasy, idle dreaming, perhaps even foolishness. Moreover, that is how they will regard the truth about Michael, who is now beginning to reveal Christ anew. Nonetheless, many people will recognize that what is just now rising is like the dawn and that what will pour into human souls in the coming centuries is like a sun, for Michael can always be compared to a sun. And even if many people will not recognize this new Michael revelation, it will nonetheless spread over humankind.

This is what can be said about the relationship of the Mystery of Golgotha, which took place at the beginning of our era and the Mystery of Golgotha as it can be understood today. Let us make these feelings our own, recognizing that it is the only way we can become true spiritual scientists. From time to time other revelations will come our way, to which we must keep an open mind. Would it not be particularly selfish to keep these feelings exclusively for our own satisfaction? Let us rather feel that it is our serious duty, as spiritual science teaches us, to make ourselves willing tools for this revelation. Although in humanity as a whole we are only a small society attempting to understand this new truth about the Mystery of Golgotha, this new revelation of Michael, we are building up a new power that does not depend in the least on our belief in this revelation, but rather depends entirely on the revelation itself, on truth itself and nothing else. Then we will recognize in all calmness that only certain among us are prepared to explain to the world, as far as it is willing to listen, that from now on there is a new manifestation of Christ. But we want to be ready to recognize it. We want to belong to that tiny circle that is willing to help it grow and become lasting. We want to build on the inner power of such a revelation, so that it may spread out among the rest of humanity, for this knowledge will eventually belong to everyone.

This is what we call wisdom. It is what many call foolishness. To be firmly present, we need only to remember today that the present time is the time of the second revelation of Michael, and to remember also what was said by one of the ancient initiates, Paul, at the time of the first revelation of Michael: "What often appears to people as foolishness is wisdom before God."

Let us try today to draw power for ourselves from feelings of this sort, from spiritual knowledge of the sort that must appear in many contexts in the external world as foolishness. Let us seize the courage to recognize that, what appears as foolishness to people who rely only on the senses, can be wisdom and light, as well as a clearer understanding of the supersensible spiritual worlds, toward which we desire to strive with all the power of our souls and our conviction.

3

The Michael Impulse and the Mystery of Golgotha (1)

Stuttgart, May 18, 1913

On my last visit here I presented, in two lectures,† some aspects of the life between death and a new birth. A perspective was chosen that kept in view the overall significance and meaning of a knowledge of the life between death and a new life, because the forces and beings a person comes into contact with there also reach into our life that runs its course between birth and death.

Today I want to begin with a wide-ranging discussion that can bring before our eyes the great mission of the anthroposophical worldview in the context of the whole character of our present cultural period. As I have often discussed in considerable depth, we are in an important segment of human development on Earth. I have emphasized quite often that even though, in an admittedly superficial consideration of the evolution of humankind on Earth, one frequently calls every period a period of transition, nevertheless, from a certain point of view, one must call our period if not exactly a transitional period, then a significant period for the entire development of humanity.

An initial perspective I would like to place before you is one I have often mentioned. In this context, we must acknowledge as always the reality that—even though its results can be studied only by the trained soul of the spiritual researcher—Anthroposophy (which we know must live its way into the human cultural life of today through necessities inherent in the development of the Earth) can be understood by any human soul, provided it is willing and brings sufficient open-mindedness to the subject.

Here the objection can easily be raised that only a few people have the kind of consciousness such that what Anthroposophy speaks of seems true to them. Moreover the majority of people consider whatever comes from spiritual science, from spiritual research, to be pure make-believe, dreaming, if not quite (as we heard yesterday†) one of "the seven sects of perdition."

What is really at the bottom of this? Given that very many people still say that they cannot understand Anthroposophy, that it seems to them to be pure make-believe, is it possible to maintain that this truth, understood by few, is still knowable by unprejudiced common sense?

In yesterday's public lecture I dealt with the problems of how one can arrive at supersensible knowledge, how one can liberate certain soul forces from their penetration into the physical. I mentioned how the forces of thinking, speech, and will can become free, can emancipate themselves from the physical so that they can function purely in the sphere of the soul and spirit, and that they are powers that can be trained through meditation, concentration, and contemplation and can then penetrate the supersensible worlds. All the forces that enable one to penetrate the supersensible worlds derive from the human ability to release the soul from everything we are tied to in a physical body. Therefore, in the powers of knowledge with which the supersensible worlds can be researched, we are dealing with soul forces that are free of the body.

Now, in ordinary, everyday life the soul already has a power that contains what the other soul forces strive for in spiritual science. This soul power is the power of thinking, as it is expressed in ordinary, unpretentious, commonsense human understanding. This power of ordinary thinking in particular can show itself under certain circumstances to be free of the body without being developed any further.

Ordinary thinking, which every soul today has within it as a power, has this special feature: it has two faces. It is Janus-headed. On the one hand, ordinary thinking is dependent on the brain and brings to consciousness only what is reflected in the brain, the nervous system. In that case, it is more passive, desiring to lean on the instrument of the brain. On the other hand, this same thinking can—without any kind of meditation—by quite simply rousing itself from within, becoming conscious of itself in its true nature, tear itself away from its dependency on the brain, free itself. Then it is a more active thinking.

Both are sides of healthy human thinking that every soul today can enjoy. Thinking is in every soul, but it can be used in a twofold way. First, human beings can gather strength in themselves and mint thoughts within themselves, in which case thinking is active and can fully engage everything—apparently even the boldest assertions of spiritual science. But when thinking does not wish to gather strength, does not wish to pull itself together in its activity, then it must lean on the instrument of thinking, the brain, and then it brings forth only thoughts that can be grasped by the instrument of the brain. In this case, the person is no longer thinking actively, but is thinking passively.

The division between active thinkers and passive thinkers is more important than any other dichotomy (not for the present, however, but for the future). Those who can form independent, free thinking in themselves, who can think actively, will be pushed forward by the force of this thinking to spiritual-scientific research. Those who are not willing to think actively, but rather only in dependence on the brain, will say that anthroposophical research is make-believe because they wish to be devoted to the instrument of the brain and have no idea of what can be encompassed by an act of thinking that is free. One could say they do not wish to think on their own, only to have the thinking done within them for their own benefit.

Precisely from this perspective one's adherence to and behavior toward the anthroposophical worldview today is basically a matter of either inner industriousness, inner strengthening, on the one hand, or of inner love of comfort, inner laziness on the other. Thinking that is willing to work hard, to strengthen itself, grasps the results of Anthroposophy; thinking that wants to avail itself of a crutch, that wants to bring thoughts to consciousness merely in the reflection of the brain—thinking that wants to be comfortable, and wants only to let thinking go on within itself—will find it necessary from its love of ease to reject anthroposophical research. All the philosophies and scribbling that flow into the world with the appearance of a scientific and intellectual character, claiming that one cannot understand what anthroposophical research can create, rest on a deep-seated, unconscious love of comfort, which does not want to become active, but rather to remain passive. Adherence to the anthroposophical worldview is not comfortable.

That is the basic truth of the matter. If you go to meetings where people, who no longer call themselves materialistic but perhaps monistic, hold forth on the "fantasies" of spiritual science, you will find that there is a good deal more to it than what is actually said in those meetings. At the foundation of such people's attitude lies the inability to progress to active thinking; and beyond that, there is the arrogance (because they will not pull themselves up to active thinking) of making the comfort of passive thinking the highest principle of human research.

The role of comfort in the use of soul forces leads in ordinary life to something one can observe quite often. Those who wish to hear this or that speech, yet are too devoted to comfort to follow the arguments, eventually doze off and sleep through what they actually came to find out, or perhaps not what they came to find out. This sort of sleeping will have to be dealt with through the necessary developmental impulses of humanity by all those people who can pull themselves together for active thinking in the present and in the near future. Some will sleep through something of the highest importance, but even though they want to know nothing about it, behind what transpires in our sense world there are supersensible beings endowed with power, supersensible processes. For that reason, although a part of humanity wishes to sleep through what is actually happening, in our present epoch we are dealing with important supersensible processes. Important supersensible processes are at stake in our age! And all sensory processes are the outer forms of supersensory processes. If we look through the veil, so to speak, in which all sensory processes of development show themselves in our epoch, we pass behind the veil to the supersensory processes. Moreover, to characterize the supersensory processes that are particularly important now, we must remind ourselves that all life in the universe rests on an ever-growing process of development.

If we pursue the human path of development, we first find human beings in the ancient Saturn period,† in accordance with their initial constitution. We then find them imbued with a new element in the ancient Sun period, still further developed in the ancient Moon period, and endowed with the fourth element, the "I," in the Earth period. And we certainly know that, in the Jupiter period, human soul forces will assume such a form that human beings will make themselves comparable to the hierarchy of the angels.

As humanity progresses in its development and rises, other beings of the individual hierarchies rise from lower to higher levels. Not only the human hierarchy undergoes such an ever-rising development, but also the hierarchies that stand above the human.

Let us take from these hierarchies the one standing two levels above human beings, the hierarchy of the archangels. I said yesterday that, from many understandable points of view, people are not particularly offended if someone speaks of spirit in general, but if one goes into classes, orders, and individuals as one does with plants, animals, and other fields of natural science, our contemporary cultured person is deeply offended. Nonetheless, one must speak in this way if we are to deal with the supersensible world in a concrete fashion.

If you pick up the cycle of lectures I gave in Kristiania on the development of different peoples,[†] you will see that their development is related to the hierarchy of the archangels. The archai, the primal forces, the spirits of personality, lie behind the successive epochs.

If we now take the most important beings from the rank of the archangels, we have names that we run into in other situations, names that we have met before: Raphael, Gabriel, Michael, and so forth. We can name these beings with such names because the name is not at all essential. We give them names in the same way that we provide other things with names. They play a certain role in what we find as the facts of supersensible development, upon which our development in the sense world depends.

Using the methods of spiritual science, we can in fact differentiate very well between the individual beings in the hierarchy of the archangels, not abstractly by merely picking names, but rather so that we can see the principle cultural impulses that manifest themselves externally in the sense world. For example we can investigate a spot of land in the first century after Christ and see it to be ruled by a different being from the one that ruled the principle cultural impulses among the leading peoples in the twelfth or thirteenth centuries, or the one that rules our own cultural development.

Let us first consider our own cultural development. In this case, we must clearly distinguish the age that began in the fifteenth or sixteenth century. Its principle signature is the rise of the natural sciences, and it brought the natural sciences to the stature we find in the nineteenth century, which cannot be admired enough.

If we take an overall view of these centuries of humankind's work in natural science, we must say that this work was led by certain peoples, who were led from within the spiritual worlds by a quite particular being from the hierarchy of the archangels, and this being is quite precisely distinct from the being who presently leads our nascent cultural epoch from the supersensible world. If we wish to give the names current in the western world for these leading beings from the hierarchy of the archangels, we can say that, starting from the time of Christ, various beings were the leaders of culture as it progressed. Without wishing to harp on these names, I will only enumerate—just as one runs through the names of people who participate in whatever process on the physical level—the names from the rank of beings in the hierarchy of the archangels who have ruled the progress of culture: Oriphiel, Anael, Zachariel, Raphael, Samael, Gabriel, Michael.

Gabriel was the leading spirit in the cultural period that has ended in the spiritual world during the last third of the nineteenth century. Indeed, in the last third of the nineteenth century, an epoch began (as has become more and more obvious) in which quite different influences and impulses flow down from the supersensible world into the sense world. While formerly human souls were predominantly directed toward what the senses see and reason can grasp, people of the age now coming, who do not wish to sleep through the development as it progresses, will have to pay attention more and more to how supersensible wisdom and knowledge makes its way from the supersensible worlds into earthly sense-bound development.

If one wishes to characterize this superficially, one could say that, in the epoch that has just ended, the supersensible beings had enough to do to keep the inspirations and intuitions that can flow in from the supersensible worlds *away* from physical life. The hierarchy played a role in preventing such intuitions and inspirations from flowing into souls. From now on, the supersensible forces will be directed and led from within the supersensible world, so that as many inspirations and intuitions as possible can flow into human souls. As a result, the human soul will be able to comprehend imagination, inspiration, and intuition. The truly living cultural impulses of the present age will be just as full of the inspired and the intuitive as the age that has elapsed was empty of any inspired nature, any knowledge of the spiritual.

It would have been impossible to say to people fifty years ago what, through the necessary course of world development, can be said to you today, because it would have been impossible then to receive these things from the spiritual worlds on Earth. The door has now been opened. And just as the past age was most favorable for the development of reason, the next age will be very favorable for the development of inspiration and intuition. Two ages are colliding hard—one that was disinclined to all inspiration, and one in which, although mighty forces will fight against all inspiration, it will be possible again to take up inspiration and make it set the tone for human souls.

If we look further into the matter, we will discover that the supersensible powers that could not flow directly into human souls in the last epoch were not quite inactive. What external physiology cannot prove is still truth. In the age of Gabriel, work emanating from within the supersensible worlds into the sense-bound world worked on the human physical body. During this time, fine structures were created within the frontal lobes of the brain that were eventually implanted by the reign of Gabriel into human generation, so that people are now born for the most part with a brain having different, finer structures in the frontal lobes than was the case with people of the twelfth and thirteenth centuries. To create these structures was the task of the Gabriel age in which people directed their intelligence toward the physical and the sense-bound, and were closed to the inspired, so that the impulses of the supersensible world poured into physicality and formed this delicate structure in the brain. Increasingly, this structure will be present in people, who will therefore feel themselves capable of moving forward to active thinking and to the understanding of spiritual science. In our epoch, at whose beginning we now stand, the supersensible powers will not be used to form structures in the brain, but rather to flow directly into human souls, to have an effect through imagination and inspiration. This is the reign of Michael.

Thus two beings in the ranks of the archangels differentiate themselves. One, Gabriel, led humankind directly before our age and worked on the finer construction of the brain. The other, the archangel who is now beginning to work, does not have the task of modifying a human organ, but rather of planting an understanding of spiritual science in human souls. This is how we can distinguish beings belonging to the hierarchy of the archangels.

In these two examples I am seeking to place before you concrete character traits of these two beings. We are cannot be satisfied only with names. Just as we know nothing about a person whose name is Miller, we know nothing about Gabriel if we know only his name. On the other hand, we know something about a person if we can say he is a sympathetic person, he has done this or that. In this way we also know something about a supersensible being when we can say that he made forces flow into the physical human body, forces that made certain structures in the frontal lobes come into being through the human power of generation. Moreover, we characterize the spirit, the being, who followed him correctly when we refer to his activity in extending the understanding for inspired and intuitive truths. Michael is at work not so much for the spiritual researcher, the initiate, as for those now and in the centuries to come who, as the powers of active thinking concentrate more and more in humanity, wish to understand spiritual science, who desire to make the transition into active thinking.

This transition is important in yet another respect. Through what happened in it, a new humanity is in the process of forming, which, through its organization, will be in a position in future incarnations to look back, through memory, to earlier incarnations. However, humanity must first put itself in this position. One cannot remember something one has never thought about. If, in the evening, a man thoughtlessly takes off his cuffs and puts down his cufflinks, he will not find them the next morning because he has not given it any thought. If he takes the idea of stamping the image of the cufflinks' surroundings into himself, the next morning he will go straight to the place where he left them.

This anecdote is not only valid for ordinary life in respect to our capacity for memory, but it is also relevant to an experience of earlier lives. We must first recall the deepest inner being of the soul—that which really passes over into the nature of the soul. But for this we must first have grasped this innermost being, which we can only do through esoteric training. If one has not made the effort to have thoughts about the nature of the soul in the earlier incarnation, one cannot remember it, no matter how well organized one may be. Although people will be organized for remembering, they will at first feel this organization as an illness, as nervousness, as a dreadful state, if they are unable to use it. They will be organized to exercise recollection, but they will have nothing to remember. If people have impressions they cannot turn to account, organs they cannot use, then they fall ill.

Compare this with the observation that people in future ages will be organized to remember earlier lives on Earth, but that only those will remember who have something to remember, who have recognized through occult training the nature of the human soul in its unique quality as a part of the spiritual world. In every life that follows a life of the sort in which one has recognized the soul as a spiritual being, there will be recollection of previous lives. So we stand at an important turning point. Understanding spiritual science means fundamentally nothing other than having a feel for this turning point in our time.

Now, not all beings belonging to the hierarchy of the archangels are similarly constructed, equal in rank. When we speak of the hierarchy of the archangels, we can say that one takes over from another, as I have said. However, the highest in rank, likewise the superior, is Michael, the one who begins to assume the leadership in our time. He is from the circle of the archangels, but he is in a certain way the most advanced. A process of development is now going on and embraces all beings. All beings are in a process of growth, and we live in the age in which Michael, the highest being of archangelic nature, is making the transition to the nature of an archai. He will gradually move into a leading position, will become the time spirit, the leading being for all of humanity.

That is what is significant. It is tremendously important in our time that we understand that what was not yet present in all previous epochs, was not available for all humanity, can now be and must become the property of all humanity. What until now appeared among individual peoples—spiritual reflection—is now accessible for the whole human race.

Moreover, just as we can speak of what is happening behind the world of the senses, we can also speak of what is transpiring in the realm of the senses as an external expression of what has just been described: that in a way an exaltation of the archangel Michael is taking place in the spiritual world.

Until now a human being could be a personality; in the future, a human being will also be able to be a personality, but in a different way than has been possible up to now. Human beings have always to a certain extent participated in the supersensible world; at least they were able to do so with their soul life. But the personal needs and personal coloring that people experienced in the sense world did not come down from above, but from below upward. It came from Lucifer—Lucifer created personality. Hence, up until now, one could have said that human beings could not penetrate into the supersensible world, could not bring their personalities into the spiritual world. They had to extinguish their personalities. Otherwise they polluted the spiritual world.

In the future, however, human beings will have to let their personalities be inspired from above, so that they can take up what should flow from the spiritual world. The personality will receive its distinctive stamp through what it can take up in the way of spiritual knowledge; the personality will become something very different in future times. To a certain extent, human beings in earlier times were personalities through what steered them away from the spiritual, through what was pushed up into them from the body. In the future, however, they will have to become personalities through what they can assimilate from the spiritual world, through what they can take up into themselves.

Through their blood, their temperament, and many sorts of things that came from below, people were actually personalities in the past, and impersonal elements radiated in into these personalities from the supersensible. In the future one will be less and less able to be a personality through temperament, blood, and so forth. But one will be able to be a personality through participation in the supersensible world. That which contains supersensible impulses will flow into character. This will aid the impulse of Michael, who leads the understanding of spiritual life right into the human soul. People in the future with a pronounced character of personality will possess this character of personality from the fact that they express this or that through understanding of the supersensible worlds.

The Alexanders, Caesars, and Napoleons belong to the past. Supersensible elements did indeed flow into them, but their high personal coloring came from what they received from below. People, personalities will now be formed by the way they carry the spiritual world down into the world of the senses. The people who carry personality into humanity from within the soul will be the personalities who will succeed the Alexanders, Caesars, and Napoleons. The strength of human deeds in the future will be produced by the strength of the spiritual elements that flow into these human deeds.

All this is part of what is significant about the transition from one epoch to the other. But just what is it that characterizes the most significant transition, the transition from the epoch of Gabriel to the epoch of Michael in our period of development?

What we have said today can perfectly well be understood with common sense if we are sufficiently free from prejudice to look into our time and see how two possibilities collide right up to the last third of the nineteenth century. The first possibility is to build a picture of the world from natural science. Today that is out-of-date. It is antiquated. It no longer fits in the character of the period. People still do it because they tend to carry on what comes from old times. The other possibility, which fits in the character of our period, is to construct a worldview from the inspirations and understanding of the spiritual world. We must take up that possibility as a feeling or sensitivity in our soul. If we do so, then we will learn what the anthroposophical worldview means for individual souls and learn to feel what development is for humanity. We will then be permitted to be participants in something significant.

Now, let me remind you of something I wove into the lectures I gave here the last time, the lectures about the alteration in the function of

Buddha.† It also is a point that should be linked to what will be said in the next lecture. Therefore I would like to close with a question, with the question that can arise in every soul and will lead us from the important issue examined today to something yet more important. When an exaltation of Michael has taken place, when he has become the leading spirit of western culture, who takes his place? The place must be filled. Every soul must say to itself: Now an angel must have experienced a promotion, an exaltation, and must enter the rank of the archangels. Who is it?

I wish to close with this question, to lead over into still more important observations that will occupy us the day after tomorrow.

Today I wanted to place before your souls the most important characteristics of the transition: the fact that the souls who can pull themselves up to it can find an understanding of supersensible truths; for the world forces that stand behind humanity and lead its evolution wish it so. And the picture of this in the sense world is that personality takes on an entirely different nuance. While in the bygone age temperament and blood gave personality its color from below, the element of spiritual understanding will give the pitch for personality in the new age. That will be the tone-giving element.

It is important to understand this, but even more important to feel it. From this point, the day after tomorrow, we will move to a significant observation that can penetrate each one of our souls.

4

The Michael Impulse and the Mystery of Golgotha (2)

STUTTGART, MAY 20, 1913

We have striven to cast a little light on what actually characterizes of our present age from the standpoint of universal laws. We should not pass over this sort of characterization of an age, for the spiritual powers and spiritual impulses of an age are the very forces and impulses at work within each of our souls. Moreover, we cannot establish ourselves on the right footing with our souls if we lack the ability to situate ourselves in relation to these forces and impulses, which in fact are simultaneously the spiritual forces and impulses of our own souls. It is altogether true that—just as each of you has established why you believe this or that in spiritual science—there also lives, even if unconsciously, in the souls of those who come to spiritual science in an upright, honorable spirit, a feeling or instinct that comes from the true impulses of our time.

The day before yesterday I sought to characterize how we presently live in what one can call the Michael age, in which understanding for spiritual things will continue to become increasingly possible for more and more souls. As the last centuries ran their course, it became possible to understand the objects of natural science and physical, chemical, physiological laws; in a word, everything pertaining to outer space and time. In that Gabriel age, understanding awoke in soul for what marched from triumph to triumph in the natural sciences, inclining them to a scientific understanding of the world. But now we are approaching an age in which it will be just as possible to understand the spiritual.

Never before in the development of humanity were two successive ages actually so radically different as the one that has just ended and the one we are entering. Souls inclined to the spiritual will seem stranger than ever to the souls who still cling to what earlier centuries brought. It will not be long until those who believe they are standing on the ground of materialistic monism will seem entirely anachronistic to souls who seek with yearning for an understanding of the supersensible worlds; for, since the last third of the previous century, a spiritual tide from the higher worlds has been opening itself to our world, making it possible to obtain understanding for what spiritually leads the evolution of humanity and the world. Almost two thousand years ago the event familiar to all of you as the Mystery of Golgotha took place, which has been discussed and illuminated here from many sides as the major center of gravity of the development of humanity. And it must have become clear that, purely from within spiritual science, without a touch of any kind of dogma, the understanding of this event is possible, so that one can expect understanding by every creed of the present day. The reasons why someone will not accept the Christ event as the major center of gravity in the evolution of humankind have also been thoroughly discussed. However, we should also examine this in relation to the kind of soul I was able to speak of yesterday in the public lecture.[†]

Someone, out of prejudice, might have no interest about what transpired in a small country at the beginning of our age. Some people may be unwilling to trouble themselves about what we call the Mystery of Golgotha. Let us even assume that it would be natural for a soul to conceive the course of history in such a way that what happened on Golgotha is erased. Let us assume it as a hypothesis. If such a soul observes the development of humankind, it would still find something that particularly characterizes this age. I discussed this yesterday. In the period before the Mystery of Golgotha, entirely independent of it, a transition took place. The transition was from the human soul's orientation toward the outer environment to an orientation toward its own intimate nature. At the moment when the Mystery of Golgotha intervened, this great transition occurred from a life in the external surroundings to a turning inward. All people can feel that, even if they ignore the Mystery of Golgotha.

Humanity at that point in time was at a crossroads. One does not need to mention the Mystery of Golgotha even once. One can take other events, which will show that previously humanity lived in an externalized state, but that afterward people begin to live in an internalized mode, which was imbued with the impulse of the time, with its genius.

When a change like that happens, it happens in a way that is prepared for beforehand. I don't wish to resort to the trivial by saying that nature never makes leaps in history. The statement is justified only within certain limits. In a plant, blossoms are also prepared among green leaves—yet isn't that a "leaping" development nonetheless? So there was a preparation for the event that took place at the time of the Mystery of Golgotha, which was a turning point in the development of humanity. But when we immerse ourselves in the teaching and outlook of ancient Hebrew antiquity in the centuries preceding the Mystery of Golgotha, it is not only there that we find a spirit, an individual spirit, who prepared for the Mystery of Golgotha, namely, an entirely new epoch in contrast to what existed in Hebrew spiritual life before then. We find such a spirit of preparation in other regions of the Earth too.

Certainly in the spirit of Judaism quite another element is present than existed before. During the sixth century before the Mystery of Golgotha, a totally different style of observing the world set in, an entirely new epoch in contrast to what previously existed in Hebrew spiritual life. That reveals itself very clearly to the precisely observing gaze. And even if it emerges here in a special way, because the ancient Hebrew people were indeed formed differently, it is still the same spirit, receiving another expression, that we find in Greece. It is the same spirit that predominates during the last centuries before the Mystery of Golgotha in Greek philosophy, indeed even in Greek poetry. We find it everywhere. One need only look seriously at spirits like Plato and Aristotle, indeed even Socrates, to see that this turning point was prepared everywhere.

Now, events of this kind occurring here on Earth will be directed and led from within the spiritual world. Before the lightning bolt that we designate as the event of Golgotha occurred in physical life on Earth, the earlier leader of evolution sent an emissary—at that time still an emissary of Yahweh—to prepare this lightning bolt. And the spirit who prepared the cultural epoch up to the Mystery of Golgotha is the same spirit who is the leader of the cultural epoch just now dawning—the spirit we have named Michael. Just as Michael gives our time its character, so he also gave character to the whole culture that prepared the Mystery of Golgotha. The only difference is that at that time the power that sent this Michael from the higher worlds was Yahweh.

It was not the same then as it is today, when one can so easily object if one talks about spiritual things: "You say a lot about the folk spirit and the time spirit and other spiritual matters, but you say so little about God." People do not notice why one does not talk about God: because no human concept can actually comprehend this being in which we live, and breathe, and do what we do every day. Here too there are opinions that are quite interesting in their way.

When I gave a public lecture recently in a city, as has now become so common, questions were offered in response, and a person asked a very clever question. He asked, "If we logically understand a thing because we look at it as an object, because we can walk up to it—while we cannot have an objective image of a thing that we have within us, like an eyeball, because we cannot look at it—how does this relate to the assertion of many mystics that one must step back from God, in order to look at him as an object?" Indeed, many mystics have proposed the statement that one must step back from God in order to stand face to face with him. The question was clever, but it must only be answered by saying, "You may step back from God as much as you like, but you remain inside of God nonetheless. You cannot get out of God." Much logic is perfectly logical, but it is also myopically logical.

In the times when people stood closer to the spiritual, one had still a feeling of reverence for the divine, in which we live, and weave, and are, and which should not always be called by name. For that reason, to avoid speaking the name, the ancient Hebrews used the expression "the Face of Yahweh." For human beings, the face is what one turns to the outside, through which one reveals oneself. It is not the whole human being, but we recognize the inner nature of a person from the features of the face; so we are not mistaken to speak of the entire human when we mean the face.

Therefore, people in those times called Michael "the Face of Yahweh;" they named rather Michael, the representative through whom, as in a face turned toward humanity, Yahweh was proclaimed to humankind. In familiar circles as well, one much preferred to name the representative rather than to speak of Yahweh himself. Michael was even then regarded as the spiritual regent of the age, as the emissary of Yahweh, as the emissary, from whom radiated what was meant to come as an impulse to prepare the event of Golgotha.

In the interval since then, other beings from the circle of the archangels have had the leadership of the spiritual evolution of humanity. And the being, who was the leader as the Mystery of Golgotha was being prepared, is the same being who now once again is sending waves of supersensible life into the sense-bound world. There was a Michael age back then, and a Michael age is just now beginning. However, there is a powerful difference between the Michael age of the past and ours that is now beginning.

It would lead us too far afield today to characterize what understanding the period that has passed by since the previous Michael age and ours would bring to the Mystery of Golgotha. There have been deeply introspective souls who, from a more or less heightened need for faith, have gained their relationship to the Mystery of Golgotha and its bearer. There have been deeply religious natures since the Mystery of Golgotha up to our times. However, the Mystery of Golgotha, which, it is true, stands as a real point of departure at the beginning of the recent age, is such that the human soul should not presume to see through it completely, just like that, to understand it. New ages will keep on coming that will continue to deepen human souls; and they will understand better and better what happened in the Mystery of Golgotha. The event itself stands as the turning point in human evolution, and understanding of it will continue to increase more and more and to ripen in the spiritual development of the Earth.

We cannot inscribe this into our souls deeply enough. Let us once grasp in our mind's eye what actually happened back then in a certain metaphysical abstraction. We have characterized it from various points of view. Now I want for once to choose a more abstract standpoint—one, however, that has the power to release in our souls, when we allow it to have its effect there, a deep feeling.

The conventional view of the world, and also conventional science, studies the things around us (I have already drawn attention to this subject yesterday in the public lecture, but we want to take another look at it). When these things are studied, a person learns through ordinary thinking and ordinary science to know the laws of existence in the mineral, plant, animal, and human realms. These laws attain their zenith in an ideal: to understand life. But life itself will not be understood here on Earth. Only esotericism can give knowledge of life. External science can never see through life. It would be the most irresponsible fantasy to believe that one can at any time see through the laws of life, as one can see through the laws of physics or chemistry. It remains an ideal, but it cannot be reached. The physical plane cannot have knowledge of life. Knowledge of life must remain reserved for supersensible knowledge.

As impossible as knowledge of life is through the senses, supersensible knowledge of death is equally impossible. There are conditions of dreadful isolation of the consciousness in the spiritual world, there is a temporary immersion as in a sleep, but there is no death in the higher worlds. Death is impossible in the higher worlds.

All beings that we have learned to know as the beings of the higher hierarchies distinguish themselves through the fact that they do not know death, that they do not undergo death. Just as it is correctly said in the Bible that the angels hide their faces before the secret of birth, of becoming human, exactly so must they and all the other higher beings also hide their faces before death. Death is an event that is possible only for the sense world, not for the supersensible.

Among all the beings of the higher worlds, only one had to go through death—we can also say, *willed* to—and that is the Christ. For that reason he had to descend to Earth.

For a higher being to accomplish this reality, which was necessary for the development of Earth, Christ had to descend from a world in which there is no death into the world in which death exists.

If such ideas are at first abstract, we must transform them into a feeling, a sensation. The full understanding of what I have just characterized abstractly will become an object of the evolution of humanity. Today, with a certain simultaneous reverence, humility, and tenderness, we draw near to the secret of the Mystery of Golgotha.

What, then, actually happened? It has often been characterized. Christ came down from the supersensible worlds into the world, in which he lives since then, albeit as a secret force, but one that will, however, manifest itself from our century on. He came down from the world in which there is no death into the world of death. And he—this power—united himself with the Earth. From being a cosmic power, he became a power of the Earth. He went through death to come back to life within the existence of the Earth, to exist within the world of the Earth. And humanity made an effort, in some souls who filled themselves with this impulse, to understand him through the centuries. However, as development moved along further in the now ended Gabriel epoch, understanding increasingly receded. And today the situation regarding that understanding is especially bad, precisely among those who should have it. Materialism not only asserts itself in contemporary materialistic science, but it also asserts itself many times over in theology. Real understanding for the Christ impulse has decreased. Materialism has seized souls, has nested itself deeply in souls.

In many respects materialism became the fundamental impulse of the last epoch, which has now run its course. Numerous souls have died and gone through the portals of death with a materialistic cast of mind. To go through the portals of death with a materialistic mentality in such a measure as souls have done in the past epoch could never have taken place in earlier ages.

In the time between death and a new birth in the spiritual world, these souls lived as if they knew nothing of the world in which they were living. A being confronted them there. They saw it in their world. They had to see it because that being had united itself with the Earth existence, even if at first it ruled invisibly in the Earth existence of the senses. And the efforts of these souls who had gone through the portals of death succeeded in driving the Christ (there is no other way for us to say it) out of the spiritual world. Christ had to experience a renewal of the Mystery of Golgotha, even if not on the same scale as previously. On Golgotha, he underwent death. Now it was an expulsion from his existence in the spiritual world. And thereby the eternal law of the spiritual world was fulfilled in him. What disappears in the spiritual world arises anew in the lower world.

If it is possible in the twentieth century for souls to develop to the point of an understanding of the Mystery of Golgotha, the possibility originates in the event by which the Christ, through a conspiracy of materialistic souls, was expelled from the spiritual worlds and transferred to the sense-bound world—the world of human beings—so that a new understanding for him could begin in the sense world as well. Thus Christ is united in a still more intimate way with everything that constitutes the destinies of people on Earth. Just as at one time one could look up to Yahweh and know that he was the being who sent Michael ahead to prepare in advance what should be carried over from the Yahweh era to the Christian era, so now it is Christ who sends Michael.

That Christ sends Michael is what is new and great and we should transform it into a feeling. As one could speak earlier of Yahweh-Michael as the leader of the era, we can now speak of Christ-Michael. Through his transformation from emissary of Yahweh to emissary of Christ, Michael has been raised to a higher level. He has been elevated from the spirit of a people to the spirit of an age.

When we speak about a correct understanding of the Michael impulse in our time, we are talking about a correct understanding of the Christ impulse.

Abstract understanding has to do with names, always with names. It believes it has something when asks, "What sort of a being is Michael?" and wants to know whether he comes from this or that hierarchy. Is he an archangel kind of being? Is he of an archangelic nature with this or that quality? Thus we define it and believe we know what such a being is. I have been asked for definitions many times. It always reminds me of the battle that took place in a Greek philosophical school about the value of a definition. There was an argument over how to define a human being. They finally came together on the point: "A human is a being that walks on two legs and has no feathers." There is no denying that these criteria apply to human beings, just as well as do many definitions apply to the concepts one stakes out in this way. On the other hand the man was right, who brought a plucked rooster to the next meeting and asked if it were a human being since it walked on two legs and had no feathers.

That is not how we should speak about Michael, especially if we wish to understand the evolution of humanity, because then we must understand Michael too in his evolution—that he is the same being who set the tone for the preparation of the Mystery of Golgotha, and now in our time sets the tone for the understanding of the Mystery of Golgotha. However, back then he was the spirit of a people; today he is the spirit of an age. Then he was the emissary of Yahweh; today he is the emissary of Christ. We are actually speaking about Christ when we speak in this way of Michael and his mission and know that he was the bearer of Yahweh's mission and is now the bearer of Christ's mission.

We have been able to follow Michael, a spirit who has risen, so to speak, in order to communicate a new impulse to humanity, who has risen, or is rising, from the rank of the archangels to the rank of *archai* or time spirit.

His place was filled by another being who comes later. I have spoken several times here about the evolution that the Buddha has undergone.[†] Those now making childish reservations against us[†] have gotten to work in their impudent way on our concept of the Christ impulse in the world, as if we have ever been one-sided with our exposition of the Christ impulse. We have trained our gaze on universal evolution, and characterized what lies beneath evolution from within different impulses. We have done justice to everyone. How often has it been emphasized that for us it is true that the bodhisattva who was born as Gautama rose up to become Buddha. We have followed his evolution to the point in time when he received his mission on Mars. We have already discussed this here.

As long as humanity remains on Earth, in the case of each person, however high his or her stature may be, we can always speak of an individuality that leads the person from incarnation to incarnation. The individual direction of human beings lies under the angels, the angel beings. If a person becomes Buddha from bodhisattva, then his angel is freed, so to speak. It is such angelic beings, who rise, after the fulfillment of their mission, into the realms of the archangelic beings.

Therefore, if we truly understand how to look deeper and deeper into what lies behind our sense-bound evolution and supersensible evolution, at one point we actually touch on the elevation of an archangel to the being of an archai and the elevation of an angelic being to an archangelic being.

I have not said what I have said to you about the spiritual background of the world in which we stand and in which we wish to place ourselves as Anthroposophists so that souls can merely theorize about these things, but rather so that souls can transform what is expressed in words and concepts into feelings. Yes, being an Anthroposophist in our day and age means to know how the supersensible world that lies at the foundation of the sense-bound world of human evolution is constituted—to feel oneself in the spiritual world as the physical human feels himself or herself physically in the atmosphere; to feel oneself in the same way in the spiritual world! However, one does not feel oneself in the spiritual world just by repeating: the spirit, the spirit, the spirit is in us! Rather, in the same way that we can form a concrete judgment of the Earth's atmosphere from cloud formations, humidity, and other phenomena, so must we also characterize *concretely* the spiritual world into which we dive every night when we go to sleep—and *feel* what lives and acts in this spiritual world.

What is happening today is happening because of the mission that has been handed over to Michael from the Christ, a mission handed down to the same archangelic spirit and by the impulse of Yahweh once used in the preparation of the Mystery of Golgotha. It is what is being played out behind our physical, sense-bound evolution. And to know oneself within it, to feel in the midst of such a process in the spiritual world as we feel ourselves physically in the atmosphere that we inhale and exhale, means today to have the right consciousness in relation to the spiritual world in a concrete sense.

Try, in an all-inclusive soul feeling, to transform these results of esotericism. Try to gain a feeling concept of what I am trying to place in your souls. Try to pay attention to what it means, particularly in this era, to live consciously within what is occurring spiritually around us and within us—where our souls go every evening when we go to sleep, and whither we come every morning when we awake. Just try to guide the soul upward in this concrete entity, often thoroughly abstractly called "divine providence."

That is in the character of our time—that what bygone peoples could feel only vaguely as providence flowing through the world, we can now recognize and feel as individual beings. Make it stand as an image before your souls that the bygone age had to find the laws of nature. At that time the laws of nature were good when they were used correctly in the human soul to construct external views of the world. But there is nothing absolutely good and bad in the outer world of maya. In our time natural laws become bad, evil, if they are further used for constructing a worldview in a time when now spiritual life flows into the sense world. These words are not meant for what bygone ages have done, but rather for that which will remain as it was in earlier ages, that which will not put itself in the service of the new revelation.

Michael did not fight the dragon in the age that has passed, for at that time the dragon that is meant today was not yet a dragon. It will become a dragon when the concepts and ideas—that are no more than laws of natural science—will be constructed into the worldview of the next age. What will seek to emerge then is correctly understood by the image of the dragon, which must be vanquished by Michael, whose age is beginning in our time.

That is an important imagination: Michael defeating the dragon, receiving flowing spiritual life in the sense world. From now on it is service to Michael. We serve him in the defeat of the dragon; the dragon seeks to produce out of itself the ideas that brought materialism in the previous age and want to grow materialism further into the future. To overcome that means to stand in the service of Michael. That is the victory of Michael over the dragon.

It is once again the ancient image, which had another meaning for earlier times but should now receive this meaning for our time. We can know and feel our duty in the image of Michael defeating the dragon when we experience what we should, as people of a new age.

So let us try to make this image part of our imagination. Let us try to understand our time through knowing that within it we are concretely in the spiritual guidance that is the spiritual guidance of our age—which can be the spiritual guidance of every human soul who uprightly and honorably seeks to develop, to rise to ever higher levels of spiritual life.

5

Christ's Path through the Centuries

COPENHAGEN, OCTOBER 14, 1913

I should like to use an aphoristic style in this evening's lecture to present something I believe is important, especially in the present time for our friends. We have often linked the observations of spiritual science to the Christ impulse, the impulse that has been active in the evolution of humanity ever since the Mystery of Golgotha took place. And I should like to tie my observations for you this evening to the Christ impulse and its significance for the development of humanity. We immediately want to emphasize that one difficulty necessarily faces us, even up to the present, in looking at this Christ impulse in the right way, because we can only really observe the Christ impulse to some extent if we ignore as much as possible the different Christian denominations, which continue to develop in our own time—to look away from the doctrines about Christ. Perhaps you will ask how we can consider the Christ impulse at all if we keep the doctrines about Christ entirely out of the picture. How else do we learn about the effects of the Christ impulse other than through the beliefs that have arisen over the centuries? We have to answer that anyone must admit that it would be wrong if one had to wait for the effects of the Sun on each individual person on Earth before a generally recognized doctrine on the Sun became widely known. The Sun functions no matter what theories people on Earth put forth about it. Moreover, science is constantly emphasizing that it does not yet know what electricity really is; yet people avail themselves of electricity. So one certainly can speak of an effect of the Christ impulse without believing that anything in the consideration of that impulse depends on what anyone has thought about Christ over the centuries. What was thought about Christ is connected with something else again.

The Mystery of Golgotha, the entry of the Christ impulse into the sphere of our Earth, was accomplished at a particular time, and the moment is determined almost exactly, since in the West we base our reckoning of time on it. Through the Mystery of Golgotha, as we know, the Christ impulse entered into the evolution of humanity. What sort of a time period was it? Now, we know that various periods in the development of humanity have elapsed. If we consider only the post-Atlantean time, we know that there have been the ancient Indian, the ancient Persian, the Egypto-Chaldean, and the Greco-Roman periods, as well as ours, in which we are still living. These different periods are characterized, among other things, by the fact that each had a different kind of human understanding, of human wisdom. In a certain way a lofty, intensive human intelligence and a high order of human insight into certain world secrets were present in the ancient Indian period. During that time, it was chiefly what we call the human etheric body working in human nature. Then in the course of evolution the etheric body withdrew more into the background, and in the ancient Persian period the sentient body, the astral body, was active; in the Egypto-Chaldean period, the sentient soul; in the Greco-Roman, the intellectual soul or mind soul; in our time, the consciousness soul; and in the future will come the age of the spirit self. Because different members of human nature prevail in different epochs, the human being always encounters the world with a different understanding of it. The human being had a different relationship to the world in each period. The relationship in the Greco-Roman period was different from that of our own; that in the Egypto-Chaldean different from the Greco-Roman, that of the ancient Persian different from the Egypto-Chaldean, and so on.

Now, we can recognize a curious fact, and this fact, astonishing as it is, is immensely illuminating. We can calculate the Greco-Roman period, the period of the intellectual or mind soul, as being from about the eighth century before Christ, roughly from the time of the foundation of Rome, up to the fourteenth or fifteenth century. When the intellectual or mind soul develops, those forces in human nature that make themselves particularly felt are those that are most connected to the soul forces of human nature. This realm of the human soul developed for two millennia. Since the fifteenth century after Christ, we have been developing the consciousness soul. We are not yet very far into it, since only when our century and then one more century have run their course will a third of the time destined for the development of the consciousness soul have elapsed. Other epochs will follow, which will awaken entirely different capabilities in the soul. There are seven such epochs in the post-Atlantean period.

Let us now ask, in which of these ages were human beings least able to comprehend the nature of Christ? The understanding inherent in human nature was of a quite different character in the different periods. Which period was least suited to acquire proper concepts of the nature of Christ? It was the age of the intellectual or mind soul, from the eighth century before Christ into the fifteenth century after Christ. And right into this period fell the Mystery of Golgotha! So strangely did this fact of the evolution of humanity take place.

Hypothetically speaking, if Christ had appeared on Earth among the holy Rishis[†] of ancient India, for example, people would have easily understood the nature of the Christ being, just as they would have in ancient Persia, where doctrines of the Sun-Spirit were taught. If Christ had incarnated in a human body then, one would have recognized this spirit walking on the Earth in a human body as the Sun-Spirit descended to Earth. For that matter, something similar could have occurred in the time of Egyptian temple wisdom. However, human beings had the least understanding of the nature of Christ during that period in which Christ appeared among them.

It is actually not easy to add anything that will shed light on this peculiar fact since we can draw the important conclusion that it is indeed obvious that hardly anything is found about the nature and being of Christ in the teachings about him in that time, and one will understand that first centuries yet to come will have more understanding for what Christ is.

The people of our age, since the fifteenth century, could begin to feel proud of our intellectual power, and believe that now perhaps better times have come for the understanding of Christ. With our fifth post-Atlantean age such times have, in a certain way, arrived, and in another way not.

What is the nature of the intellectual powers of present humanity, that is, of humanity living since the fifteenth century? In general these spiritual powers have in no way become more elevated than they were in earlier periods. In a certain sense human beings and everything pertaining to their souls have sunk even deeper into matter, which is also necessary for the development of the consciousness soul. So we see how the spiritual science, which was preserved in memory before the fifteenth and sixteenth centuries, disappeared and how materialism increased. We see the retreat of the spiritual science, which we find flourishing in a certain way in individual spirits of the Middle Ages, and which, so to speak, reached a certain height as if out of the elemental nature through the mystics. From the eleventh and twelfth centuries on, on the contrary, we see the preparation of a new development, a symptom of which is that people begin to prove the existence of God. Now, we must have very peculiar opinions about the world if we don't quickly perceive what that means. What do we need to prove? Usually what we don't know, what isn't familiar! We attempt to prove that a person has stolen, if we haven't seen him or her commit the theft. When people lost the inner experience of God, when they no longer knew on which path of the soul one should look for God, they began to prove God. This is an incontrovertible proof that one has begun to lose the knowledge of God. The fifth age[†] must be the materialistic age, because only through the human beings of this time being compelled to look at nature with the senses and the intellect, in order to overcome it through the senses, can the "I" become consciousness with all its strength.

If we want to come to an understanding about what I really mean, then we should to refer back to the ancient Persian age. In the ancient Indian age, that which I wish to point out would have shown itself even more clearly, and in the Egyptian period it was still there in a certain way. To a person of the ancient Persian culture it would have seemed very strange to observe the movement of the planets and to derive from it a system of the universe like that of Copernicus. And now I must say something quite paradoxical. People of the ancient Persian culture would have been astonished if someone had wanted to teach them astronomy of the present sort. A person of that time would have said, "Am I really such a fool that, if I want to walk, someone has to show me how to walk? When the Sun follows its path through space, my soul goes with it. I really have to say that." People then knew this, just as we know today what path we are taking when our body is walking. With the old knowledge the ancient Persians drew a spiral, which truly corresponds to the course of the Sun through space. This course of the Sun was found through an inner perception. The human soul felt itself connected with the soul of the Earth and indicated the path of the Earth with the caduceus of Mercury. Later on human beings became so cast out from their spiritual environment that they had to continually fuss over and calculate the path of the Earth as the path of a planet.

On the other hand, if human beings had remained the same in relation to the external world, they would never have been able to arrive at full self-consciousness. They would have gone through the Greco-Roman cultural period and the intellect and mind would have been left on their own, wallowing around in themselves, so to speak. A condition would have arisen in which the soul would no longer know directly how it stands in relation to the world; rather it would make progress only in itself. Here too, human souls had to come out of the old relationship to the outer world and enter the age of the consciousness soul. Human beings must learn to live in their "I" and only in their "I." They should show everything external as separated from their "I," and everything should be known only through logic. Thus human beings were cast out of the spiritual content of the world.

In the Greco-Roman world the soul still had within it the direct active principle of the intellect that no longer experienced processes directly in the external world. It did have, however, God within it. In the new age human beings also lost God within. Aristotle would never have thought of proving God, because the intellectual or mind soul still experienced God within itself. The intellectual or mind soul could not prove Christ, but it still had God within it. Then, from the fifteenth or sixteenth century on, God too was lost. Despite this loss, human beings will still be able to come directly to an idea of God through their own power.

So we have had for four hundred years, from the fifteenth century on, the human intellect, which, left on its own, can never penetrate the idea of God. Within this period, something very curious occurred, which has been held very much against us, because we noticed it. The philosopher Immanuel Kant† lived at the dawn of this period, in the eighteenth century, and nothing less happened to Kant than that he confused the individual character of the human soul since the fifteenth century with the universal nature of the human soul itself. From that position he came to the odd conclusion that human beings can never arrive at a knowledge of God from within themselves—while he really should only have said that this is impossible only since the beginning of the fifteenth century. But as Lucifer had a good grip on his collar and made him an arrogant fellow, he believed that it was true for the entire human race.

Now, one could then say that the prospects for the knowledge of the Christ being must be even worse than in bygone centuries. That is, however, not the case. For humanity has still other faculties of knowledge than it had back then in the fourth post-Atlantean cultural period or than those now exclusively used to understand the "I" fully. These other powers of knowledge lie more in the ground of the human soul and must first be brought to the surface. However, people of today do this only when forced to. As long as human nature had the possibility of arriving at the knowledge of God on the surface, people made no further effort to penetrate to their deeper powers. Now, however, since human beings in our own age cannot approach God, they are compelled in reaction to dig deeper into themselves and bring up forces other than those that lie on the surface of human nature. This is connected with the fact that we are encountering a time when a knowledge of the Christ Being, based on the deeper powers of human nature, is beginning to take hold.

A few days ago in Kristiania I had the privilege of speaking about a "fifth Gospel."† It contains communications about the Christ being that are not available in the other Gospels. From the fifth Gospel one learns still other things about the Christ being than is in the other four Gospels, which leads us even more into the nature of this being. In speaking such things about the nature of the Christ being, which are to a certain extent new, there can be fundamentally no talk of committing an immodest deed, for one only communicates such things when the times demand it. But also, for example, what has been said here in Copenhagen about the Christ being and is available in print in *The Spiritual Guidance of the Individual and Humanity* and in various lecture cycles belongs already to this fifth Gospel in a certain way. Such things are said when the times urge that humanity learn of them. If you take only the one point about the two boys named Jesus discussed in *The Spiritual Guidance of the Individual and Humanity*,† you will admit that the powers of the soul that today constitute understanding are not very deep and not only fail to understand these things, but rage mightily against them when they are spoken of.

We stand, therefore, before a new kind of concept of Christ, which will in fact not be easily understood. It will be possible to understand it, but it will be found through more deeply lying soul powers. If one wants a sort of preview, with the vision of clairvoyant research, of the future of humanity in the coming centuries, as well as in the coming reincarnations of people living now, then it must be said that the soul powers lying on the surface become ever weaker. Humanity will feel itself more and more dependant on the revelations of the deeper soul forces.

The Greco-Roman period is justifiably extolled, because the people who lived rightly in it had a certain inner containment of their being. This can no longer be the case with healthy soul natures today and in the future will be even less so. If in the future we were to teach humanity only what can be researched with the powers lying on the surface, then people would become desolate in their souls. They would become desolate in a remarkable way.

Today we have not come so far that religious traditions are no longer taught in school,† but many demand already that only the fruit of natural science be taught. The demands of these people for external life will indeed become so powerful, that in a very short time humanity will be superficial to a monstrous extent. Today people still learn how to write. In a near future, human beings will have only a memory that people in earlier centuries once wrote. There will be a kind of mechanical stenography, which will be machine-written to boot. Mechanization of life! I will only indicate it through a symptom: imagine the peak of a culture in which people will excavate the historical truth that once there were human beings who had handwritten manuscripts, just as today we excavate what is found in the Egyptian temples. People will excavate handwritten manuscripts, as we excavate the monuments of the Egyptians. However, a reaction of soul life against it will also appear. And, as true as it is that our handwriting will be for the future something similar to what hieroglyphics are for us, something that human beings will be amazed at, it is equally true that human souls will also press to receive the direct revelations of the spirit again. External life will become superficial, but the inner life will demand its due.

People may now scorn what we practice today as spiritual science, but the materialists will have to retreat before the yearning cry of people for the spiritual world. And then in those periods, which will have an open mind for spirituality people will begin to recognize Christ, certainly through a reaction against external life.

In order to get a clearer picture, let us look at the problem from another angle. Perhaps your souls will resonate with the following: We can look at the image of the women who, according to scripture, go to find Christ's corpse, and find the opened tomb, but no corpse. They find the angel who says, "He whom you seek is no longer here. He is risen!" He lives in the spirit; for he, whom they had sought in matter, afterward appears to and teaches the apostles, those exceptional people who had attained a receptivity and an understanding for him. Thus Christ appeared in spiritual form. And he traveled in the spirit through Greece, Rome, up as far as the Germanic peoples, from east to west and from there northward.† And we shall not seek an understanding, an idea, a conceptual, scientific understanding of the Christ being from the great Roman philosophers, who truly speak of Christ as they would of something they do not understand. But we also will not find an understanding of the Christ among, so to speak, the stammering Germanic peoples; Christ, who lives only in their hearts, enraptures their souls but is not truly understood.

And when we enter the eleventh, twelfth, or thirteenth century, it is not the women who go to the tomb to seek the body of Christ and do not find it—the corpse which could be physically understood; now it is whole flocks of European peoples who journey to his grave. We come to the times of the Crusades, in which the crusaders travel from west to east to the tomb where once the women went. And what do these multitudes who make the pilgrimage to the tomb see? They experience: "What you seek is not here!" In truth, what they sought sprang from the mind, from what lived in their souls, but they understood it so poorly that they traveled to the East to look for the physical grave. And after a long series of disappointments and much suffering, they learned, "He whom you seek is not here!" What was it, then, that they were seeking?

We see on the one side the Crusades to the East and, on the other, European mysticism preparing itself in Tauler and Meister Eckhart, and later reaching a peak in Jakob Böhme.† The one they went looking for in the East and failed to find *was* here! He had died there; yet, he lived here in a peculiar way. When we enter into the topic of the mysticism of the Middle Ages, what is its most significant trait? These spirits, Eckhart, Tauler, and the others, make no claim to understand God or Christ, but they wish, as they say, to live a very "peaceful" life, in order to experience Christ in their soul. And the more they experienced Christ in themselves, the more they knew that they desired to be penetrated with the Divine, with Christ in the sense of their times. The Crusaders had only received the information, "He whom you seek is not here!" That which they had sought came to life again in the form of European mysticism.

Once again, we live in a peculiar age. Not only the European peoples, but also the peoples of America have a share in what we experience. The remarkable drama that we can experience can show itself in thousands and thousands of symptoms. Let me characterize only one of them, from Berlin. On the first of February 1910, a renowned, modern theologian† spoke the following "brilliant" sentence: "Ladies and gentlemen, I ask you, show me one single sentence that is reported to belong to Jesus Christ which I cannot prove was already alive in pre-Christian spiritual life." This is so very typical of the style of the present day. People prove that what is contained in our Christianity was already there before, even the entire Lord's Prayer. This theologian makes thus a pronouncement entirely in the spirit of our time, and we will hear this sort of thing more and more. What sort of an impression are we to have if we hear such a gentleman maintain that all of Christ's sayings were already there before? I once heard a very well-read person give a lecture at which a child was in attendance. When asked, "What did you hear?" the child answered, "He didn't tell me anything new. I knew all the words already!" That is how the theologian listens to every sentence and hears nothing new that might resound through the sentences.

These things should really be obvious, but nonetheless in the present day they are only taken up with opposition. People believe that if they are educated, then their knowledge is complete; in fact, the attitude is widespread that educated people can judge everything for themselves. With such a mind-set, we have experienced an unusual drama. As materialism gained in influence in the last centuries, there arose a disinclination among people to speak of Christ Jesus as such; a version of theology arose that discarded every aspect of divinity from Jesus Christ, so that he is only spoken of as Jesus, a human being, albeit a human being of high stature. This tendency in theology progressed quite far in the nineteenth century. In 1863, this theology received grotesque expression in Ernest Renan's famous work, *The Life of Jesus*. The author relates beautiful things about Jesus in a beautiful language. However, he describes already the miracle of Lazarus as if Jesus had not really awakened a person who had died, but rather authorized his followers to tell the story as if he had performed such a miracle. Therefore, this miracle was really a concession to his followers, a sort of hocus-pocus or fraud. So in this otherwise truly handsome work, something gets mixed in that smacks of a cheap novel. It is a question why Renan uses such admiring words for a man who, as he describes him, is not all that admirable. However, for half a century people have simply accepted this attitude without thinking. Renan's work is only one example from a literature that sees Jesus Christ as nothing more than a human being.

Now people have made the peculiar discovery that much that is reported about this Jesus Christ would be impossible if Jesus Christ had been an ordinary human being, especially the saying that Jesus considered himself to be the Christ, that is, not a mere human being. There we run into much that is not true. In recent times people found information that put God back in the place of the human—however, a God that was merely thought or imagined. There Christ Jesus appears as a shadow, a schema, a fetish—like a spiritual fetish, however. What a curious drama! For centuries people had forced the God out of Jesus Christ and made a human being of him, and now we experience that God once again makes the mere human being impossible. And things will continue this way, showing sufficiently that we are on a track on which understanding is impossible for the powers that lie on the surface. People in the twentieth century have attempted a sort of crusade to seek the historical Christ Jesus. And once again the answer will come: "He whom you seek, you shall not find here." For those who look for the historical personage of Jesus in this way will not be able to find him any more than could the women at the tomb or the crusaders who made the pilgrimage to the tomb. Just as the crusaders could not find Christ because they did not seek him within themselves, contemporary crusaders cannot find Christ Jesus because they do not seek him with the powers that lie within the human soul, because they do not turn to the spiritual powers that alone can find the Christ.

A deepening of the forces of spirit and soul is being prepared in the womb of the spiritual current of thought. And while the mental powers on the surface will increasingly deny the Christ, deeper spiritual powers will appear and will seek the Christ more and more. An increasing number of people will see Christ, as he enlivens the etheric sphere and is found by people who are receptive. For that reason we speak of an etheric existence of Christ in the twentieth century. We will then know from our own experience that at the Mystery of Golgotha the being called the Christ truly entered the earthly sphere, and more and more people will know who Christ is, for they will see him.

Acquaintance with spiritual science will deepen souls to the point that human vision will awaken for the Christ. A wonderful perspective opens up for clairvoyant-prophetic vision! The soul powers that lie on the surface will become increasingly insufficient, and people will eventually be born who will be done with these superficial soul powers relatively quickly. However, an age will soon approach that will remind us of the Christ event in a remarkable way.

In the thirtieth year of his life Jesus of Nazareth saw the Christ enter into himself. A new soul life began in the body of Jesus of Nazareth, because the Christ entered him and replaced the Zoroaster "I," which left him. That was at the beginning of our time reckoning. An age now approaches in which the people will become ever more numerous in whom, from the thirtieth year of their lives on, Christ knowledge will enter them, as if through enlightenment. It is not Christ in his entirety, but is Christ knowledge. In the thirtieth year of life a new comprehensive soul life will begin for these people, because they will see Christ in his etheric nature.

We understand our time in the sense of the spiritual science if we acquire understanding for this perspective. When souls living now incarnate again (many of whom will be reborn sooner than usual), many will feel from an earlier age than was previously the case that something has entered their life through inner beholding that they would only have known through instruction before. They will be able to say, "Inner vision has entered my life, and now I know for myself who the Christ is. I have achieved understanding through my inner vision." Then people will no longer want to prove Christ, because an increasing number of people can report that they find Christ wandering about the Earth as a spiritual being. People will no longer seek merely the historical Christ.

This image of the future has two sides: on the one side, a desolation increasingly emerging through the soul powers that lie on the surface, and on the other side, precisely through the reaction against this desolation, a summoning of the soul powers that lie in the depths. We disseminate Anthroposophy in order to bring about a knowledge of this image.

People should not allow the quiet, faint impressions they receive to pass by unnoticed, for only rarely will vehement impressions occur. True Anthroposophy will help human souls to recognize enlightenment so it will not pass by unnoticed; otherwise they would not be able to receive it for several incarnations. Others however, out of their superficial soul forces, will denounce those who have received enlightenment as fools, as insane people. A first step in this direction has already been made in a dreadful way. Psychiatrists have already thrown themselves into the research of Jesus Christ, studying the Gospels as symptoms of insanity. We should not pass by such phenomena without paying attention. We should rather gain the insight that the other side urgently requires attention: the side that presents an understanding of the Christ, who entered humanity at a time when he could be least understood and who continues to prepare the way for an understanding that will come in future times.

The person who looks into the future should not dismiss, with an abstract, general phrase, that which will appear in the future. The future shows itself from two sides: from the side of desolation, the rising of materialism, and also from the side of being born in a new spiritual world, not only in thoughts (or, rather, let us say opinions) but as something existential; for Christ will walk by the side of human beings and become their counselor. This is not meant simply as a metaphor; people will receive the advice they need from the living Christ, who will be their advisor and friend, and who will speak to human souls like a person who walks beside them. If humanity needed a prophetic announcement when Christ appeared physically in a human body, we need one even more now, when he will come in an etheric manifestation. Let us consider therefore what has been said as a preparatory prophecy of that which will come and must come.

Have no illusions about the future. However, we will form no illusion about the future, if we hold before us what external material life looks like, if we take as our point of departure the observation that in the future one will speak of handwriting as we talk about the hieroglyphics of the ancient Egyptians. There is still a last remnant of a spiritual cultural; a physiognomy of the soul still appears in our handwriting. However, soon this trace of the spiritual will have disappeared as completely as has Egyptian culture for us today. We will speak of much that still pertains to the soul as of something long past. The same mouth that will announce that there was once such a thing as human handwriting will announce, out of the spiritual side of things, that Christ is alive in spirit and once again walks about among human beings. People will have to exchange the spirit of mere thinking for the spirit of direct vision, of direct compassion and shared experience of the Christ who is spiritually alive and walks at the side of all human souls.

6

The Three Spiritual Preliminary Stages of the Mystery of Golgotha

Stuttgart, March 5, 1914

Following up from the considerations on the fifth Gospel,† today we will contemplate the effect of the Christ spirit on the development of the human being as it was accomplished in the spiritual worlds before the Mystery of Golgotha.

As we do this, we must remember the fact of the two Jesus children: the Solomon boy, in whom the Zoroaster "I" lived, and the Nathan boy. We must look at the Nathan Jesus boy and ask ourselves what sort of a being this boy was in whom the "I" of Zoroaster later entered.

To understand this being, we must go far back in the development of the Earth and the human being. This being who was active in the Nathan Jesus boy entered a physical incarnation for the first time in Jesus of Bethlehem. Before that it had participated in the development of humanity from within the spiritual world, but had never lived in a physical human body. It had lived along with humanity in this way through the epochs in which the human sheaths were formed, lived through the Saturn age in which the seed of the physical body was established, in the Sun and the Moon ages when the etheric and the astral bodies took form, and lived also through the smaller stages that repeat the great epochs of time. However, as the human "I" descended in the Lemurian age into the three sheaths, this being stayed behind in the spiritual worlds as, in a manner of speaking, a part of divine human existence and did not participate in the development of the "I" in the three sheaths and its seduction by the luciferic-ahrimanic attack. This being that stayed back in the spiritual world descended for the first time into a physical body as the Nathan Jesus boy, in order to let himself be illuminated by the Christ. The baptism by John represents the penetration of Jesus by the Christ spirit.

However, that was not the first time that part of divine human existence allowed itself be infused with the Christ. While living in the spiritual worlds as a spiritual being, it was already capable of being penetrated repeatedly by the Sun-Spirit. To prepare the Christ event in the physical body, something similar was accomplished in the spiritual worlds and worked into the development of humanity.

Let us look back to the Lemurian period, when the human being bound itself with its sheaths, and see how the being of the human being would have formed itself if only the forces of the cosmos with which it was connected at the time had worked on it. There was a danger at that time that the twelve cosmic forces at work on the human being might lapse into disorder. Because of this disorder, the human would have had to develop in a totally different fashion than is the case today. The senses of the human being, which were taking form back then, would have become hypersensitive under the influence of the powers about to lapse into disorder. The present-day human being can calmly take in light sensation, all perception. Under the influence of the luciferic-ahrimanic attack, the life of the senses would have released the most powerful desires and impulses. For example, if human beings saw the color red, as would have been the primary effect of the rays of the Sun, the soul, filled with desire, would have had to flee in burning pain, and with the perception of blue, the soul would have been consumed within with agony.[†] The soul would have had to suffer terribly with every sense impression, driven from animalistic passion and desires to scorching pain and torture.

Then the agonized scream of tortured humanity made its way up to that spiritual being (that being which would later incarnate in the Nathan Jesus). The scream of humanity drove this being to the Sun-Spirit, so that it could let itself be infused with the Christ. Through this infusion, the inner power of sense perception was made milder and the most powerful temptation of Lucifer and Ahriman was repulsed. Because it reduced the excessively strong effect of the forces on the senses, it transformed perceptive life into a moderate passivity.

Let us proceed further, into the Atlantean period. There a new danger hovered over human beings: through the luciferic-ahrimanic influence, the life processes, the life organs of the human were threatened. For example, the presence of food would have awakened an animalistic desire to gulp it down. The soul would have been nothing but desire. Breathing would have been especially sensitive. Bad air would have filled the human being with shuddering disgust. Everything associated with nutriment and life functions would have released a monstrous goading of sympathy and antipathy; it would have driven the soul from voracious desire to repelling disgust.

And once again it was that spiritual being who turned away this danger for human beings. For a second time it let itself be infused with the Christ spirit, and thereby rescued the human life forces, which would otherwise have lapsed into disorder.

At the end of the Atlantean epoch, a third danger arose for human beings through the luciferic-ahrimanic influence. There was a danger that the human soul forces, thinking, feeling, and willing, would lapse into disorder, into disharmony in relation to each other, so that the three forces would no longer harmonize properly in the human soul. Glowing with passion, the human being would have followed every impulse, or, filled with fear or hate, would have flown from it, without reason having the possibility of regulating the forces. How did this spirit being bring help? It had to dive into the passion-filled human soul, and become the passion itself; it had to become a dragon, in order to transform the soul forces by letting itself be illuminated by the Christ spirit for a third time.

We find this spiritual happening reflected in the myths of all peoples, for example, in the myths of St. George and of the archangel Michael defeating the dragon. In post-Atlantean cultures we see a lively awareness of the interventions of Christ accomplished in the spiritual world through that spirit being. In the Zoroaster cult we encounter the lofty Sun being, and in the Greek consciousness, an image of it appears in the Apollo service. The temple of Apollo stands by the Castalian Spring, where well-prepared Greeks would go to gain counsel from Apollo. Python, who slumbers above the steamy clouds rising from the cleft and encircling Mount Parnassus like a serpent, is vanquished by Apollo, and in his place comes Pythia, the priestess, through whose mouth Apollo reveals his wisdom to the Greeks. From spring to autumn, Apollo sojourns in his seat, and then travels north to the land of the Hyperboreans. Apollo must travel north as the spirit of the Sun while the physical Sun moves to the south. We find Apollo connected with music, with playing the lyre, representing the harmonizing of the three human soul forces. And it is said of a famous man with oversized ears, King Midas, that Apollo made ass's ears grow on him as a punishment for his decision against Apollo in the musical contest between Apollo and Marsyas, because King Midas preferred Marsyas's flute to Apollo's lyre-playing.

Three times, therefore, before the Mystery of Golgotha occurred, did Christ connect himself with humanity from within the spiritual worlds, through the threefold penetration of the spiritual being that was later the Nathan Jesus boy: first in the Lemurian epoch to regulate sense experience, second at the beginning of the Atlantean period to regulate the life forces, and third at the end of the Atlantean period to regulate the soul forces. Only then, as the fourth intervention, the Mystery of Golgotha was accomplished to regulate the "I" in its relation to the world.

The danger for the human "I," into which it was led by the temptations of Lucifer and Ahriman, was felt in advance in the Egyptian priest centers, in the Greco-Roman period. Human beings felt the "I" approaching and sought to wrestle with the forces desiring to bring it into disorder. At that time one saw in the temples at many places ceremonies somewhat like this often repeated: the priest formed a hideous, misshapen object—a crocodile—spat on it, threw it to the ground, and burned it. Other priests told the people that Ra, the divinity of the Sun, followed his course from east to west, and in the West he faded and fell down, because he had to fight against demonic beings.

Human beings felt the forces of the "I" pushing outwards. We encounter this in a twofold form. We see the Sibyls appear in the seventh to the eighth centuries and travel throughout the southern European countries. In these Sibyls there lived something that revealed the possibility of the forming of the "I." This phenomenon, however, was connected with the elemental forces of the Earth, which work in the subconscious of the soul and push themselves out in a passionate manner. In contrast to the Sibyls stands the prophecy of the Hebrew people. The prophets wanted to suppress anything sibylline in their souls, and to listen only to the revelations that open up to the conscious forces of the "I." Michelangelo depicts the prophets immersed in meditation, and across from them and in contrast with them, he depicts the Sibyls with elementary forces of the earth, connected with wind, fire, and air.

Without the Mystery of Golgotha, the sibylline element would have prevailed over and suppressed the conscious "I" forces. The "I" would have been lost to the development of humanity. We see the Christ impulse at work as a force in the course of humanity, even without human consciousness of it, as a power that forms cultures, that forms the history of the European peoples, and that determines the shaping of Europe. On the twenty-eighth of October of the year 312, Constantine defeated Maxentius. Maxentius had consulted the Sibyls and received the answer: "If you bring your army out in front of the gates of Rome, you will defeat Rome's greatest enemy." Directly afterward, Maxentius had had a dream, and he followed the utterance of the Sibyl and the dream. He marched out before Rome against all reason and against the advice and all the plans of his generals. Constantine also had a dream: he saw how, carrying the banner of Christ before him, he prevailed over his opponent who was four times stronger. Against all human reason, the battle took place, and Constantine won, carrying the cross before his army.

We can look at the historical course of humanity from 800 B.C.E. to our own time. In the centuries before Christ, we see the deep wisdom of the Greeks rise to its highest point. In this time humanity exhausts the last inherited powers of the gods. Then, at point zero, the Mystery of Golgotha occurs and works into humanity. After the Mystery of Golgotha, the stimulating powers of the Christ impulse had a different effect; they went out from different levels of the spiritual world.

	I	II	III	IV
0-800	Higher spirit world			
800-1600		Lower spirit world		
1600-2400			Soul world	
2400-				Physical world

Dividing it up, we can first grasp the time of the first eight centuries after Christ. We saw how human reason failed in relation to the Christ impulse (Gnosis†), and yet, how this Christ impulse had its effect in human events (Maxentius and Constantine). In the first eight centuries, the power of the Christ impulse worked into the physical world from the highest spiritual worlds, from the upper devachan.† We find a transition, a conclusion of this period, in the works of Scotus Erigena,† around 850 C.E. In his system of thought the Christ impulse still functions as a wave of power from the highest spiritual world into the physical.

Then, from 800 to 1600 C.E., the Christ impulse works from lower devachan into the physical world. People seek to bring this impulse close to them in ideas and in forms of many kinds. However, thought proves to be clumsy, the efforts fruitless. Neither the Crusades nor the attempts to prove the existence of God can produce a living connection.

At the transition to the next period stands the Maid of Orleans.† The impulses of Christ were revealed to her soul from the spiritual worlds. Through her, they intervene in the shaping of the history of humanity.

The force that asserts itself in the human being directly from the high spiritual realms is disappearing more and more. The forces are becoming ever weaker. From 1600 C.E. on into our time, the Christ impulse works only from the astral world, the soul world; hence, theology becomes increasingly more erudite and abstract. It puts the "simple man from Nazareth" in the place of the cosmic divine being. Our time would have progressed much deeper into materialism, would have been penetrated even more strongly by the anti-Christian element, if the forces of Christ working from the astral world had not still asserted themselves in a special way. In the fifteenth and sixteenth centuries, remarkable tales appeared everywhere, which were disseminated throughout Western Europe. In the most diverse places in all the countries of Europe, men came, with feet covered with calluses, in wretched garb, with long, flowing hair. They told of being present at the Mystery of Golgotha and of having seen Christ wander the Earth. However, as he had passed by their house, they had showed him no reverence; they had offended him. Hence, they were obliged, since that time, to roam about constantly without rest or peace, and to tell, as penance, what they once experienced (Eternal Jew). They told the whole story as if from memory. They were taken in everywhere, received by bishops and prelates. Insight into the akashic chronicle lived in these men, and they could do nothing throughout their lives other than appear in this way, and bear witness to the Christ impulse. The rest of their consciousness was dimmed; but through the impulses from the astral world they could achieve this vision. Through these occurrences, human beings were saved from the clutches of anti-Christianity and the worst materialism.

From 2400 C.E. on, the epoch will come in which the powers for understanding Christ will come from the Earth alone, when the Christ will work on human beings from within the physical plane. However, the harbinger of what will become substantial after 2400 reaches into our time: Christ will reveal himself on the physical plane in etheric form. And so we see history unfold from one period of eight hundred years to the next, in relation to impulses from the spiritual worlds. In my book *World and Life-Views of the Nineteenth Century*, and as it is expanded in the new version called *The Riddles of Philosophy*, you will be able to pursue the development of human consciousness in the same periodic steps.

The history of human thought life shows us that, if the necessary forces for the future understanding of Christ are be there, thinking itself must go through a transformation. Today we see the life of thinking inserted between two views, and the human being suffers from "being squashed in between" and cannot find a way to get from one perspective to the other. On one side stands Haeckel, who regards only external perception as valid and who produced a picture of reality and the world that cannot recognize the reality of thought. On the other side stands Hegel, who proceeds from thought as spiritual reality—the life and activity of thinking in truth is the active spirit—and who constructs a thought-picture of the world, which his contemporaries cannot recognize as reality. What thought needs is that people let it become a living reality.

It is necessary to form thoughts as living beings, like the seed of a plant. Seeds can be sowed, harvested, and then used for nourishment. Through that process, they stray from their real path, which is to let new plants sprout from the seed. In like manner, people have collected thought seeds in the granaries of natural science and philosophy, have piled them up and let them dry out. If it is supposed to come to new sprouting, the plant seed must, according to its nature, be sunk into an enlivening environment. Thus it is necessary to sink Hegel's thought seeds into the ground of spiritual science; there they can mature into fruit-bearing life, to the spiritual faculties of imagination, inspiration, and intuition. In the place of the categorical imperative, the "I" will set in motion "moral imagination,"[†] from out of the power of awakened thinking. Then it will be possible to understand the coming Christ impulse from out of the earthly powers. That is the connection between the world of thought in *The Philosophy of Freedom* and the higher powers of knowledge arising in our soul through the paths shown by spiritual science.

In connection with the coming Christ event, I have found it necessary to speak to you today about enlivening thinking for future knowledge of the spirit.

7

The Christ Impulse across the Ages and Its Power in the Human Being

Pforzheim, March 7, 1914

IN our time it becomes increasingly important for souls, whose karma has led them to spiritual science, to receive a deep impression of the meaning of the Mystery of Golgotha. Friends who were present at our most recent branch meetings have already heard much about the fact that the Mystery of Golgotha has a prehistory. It is, as it were, the conclusion of a series of events. These dear friends have also heard that, in the Earth's development, the Christ being united with the body of Jesus of Nazareth. Through this union, a being walked on fields of earth through whom the presence of the cosmic Christ being was revealed within earthly existence.

It is important for the whole future development of humanity that human beings today acquire an increasing understanding of the Mystery of Golgotha. From this understanding, reverence and deeply heartfelt devotion must flow toward what occurred through the Mystery of Golgotha for the development of humanity. As we have said repeatedly, we know that, in the preparation for the Mystery of Golgotha, two Jesus infants were born. One was the Jesus with the Zoroaster "I"; the other, from the Nathan line of the house of David, was a most special being. We know that, when the Nathan Jesus was twelve, the Zoroaster "I" moved over into him from the other boy, the Solomon Jesus.

Between his twelfth and thirtieth years, this Nathan Jesus, bearing the Zoroaster "I," prepared to undergo the event shown in the baptism in the Jordan—the reception of the Christ being. The Christ being interpenetrated this Jesus of Nazareth and, at death, poured itself out into the spiritual sphere of the Earth. As a result, humanity can participate more and more in the spiritual powers proceeding from the Mystery of Golgotha—powers that can flow through all souls and hearts.

I have already said that, before Golgotha, in a certain way as preparation, the Mystery of Golgotha took place three times for the salvation of humanity: once in the ancient Lemurian age, then in the Atlantean age, and then once again toward the end of the Atlantean age. Finally, at the beginning of our time (as we reckon it in the post-Atlantean period), it took place for the fourth time in the way we know it. Only what we call the Mystery of Golgotha took place on the physical plane. The other events, which were preparatory ones, took place entirely in the spiritual world. But what happened then—the forces that formed—flowed down into earthly souls and bodies for the salvation of humanity.

In all the events that prepared the Mystery of Golgotha, the same being, which was born later as the Nathan Jesus, was suffused with the Christ being. The essential aspect of the Mystery of Golgotha is that this Jesus being who grew up as the Nathan boy was permeated by the Christ being. The being, who later became the Nathan Jesus, was also present at the three earlier events, only then he was not incarnated as a physical human being. He lived as a spiritual, archangelic-like being in the spiritual worlds, and was interpenetrated by the Christ being in the preliminary stages of the Mystery of Golgotha, during the Lemurian age and twice during the Atlantean age.

Consequently, we can say that there were, so to speak, three angelic lives in the spiritual world. The being who led this angelic or archangelic life was fundamentally the same one who was born later as a human being and is described in the Gospel of Luke as the Jesus child. Three times this angelic being, who later offered himself for sacrifice as a human being, offered himself for interpenetration by the Christ impulse. Just as we have in Christ Jesus a human being suffused with the Christ impulse, we can also say that previously an angel was interpenetrated with the Christ impulse three times. And just as what happened through the Mystery of Golgotha flowed out into the spiritual atmosphere of the Earth, so also what occurred in the first three events flowed out of the cosmos onto the Earth. If we look at the course of human evolution— and see how the Mystery of Golgotha stands at the midpoint of human development—we can, in fact, say that the Mystery of Golgotha is such a midpoint in earthly development. Everything that happened before the Mystery of Golgotha points ahead, and prepares for the Mystery of Golgotha. And everything that happened afterward represents the gradually progressing flow of the forces from the Mystery of Golgotha into human souls and hearts.

If we look more closely into which part of the human being received what flowed out from the force of the Mystery of Golgotha, we can say that the force of the Mystery of Golgotha flows to that part of the human being that can develop its consciousness in the physical world. Is that not so? We cannot yet speak of Jesus Christ to the child who has just been born. There is no way we can make a child understand who or what Jesus is. If we could look into the soul of a child whose eyes are resting on some image, whether an image like the Sistine Madonna or the crucifix, we would notice that we cannot approach a child at the very beginning of life with the outer pedagogical methods we use on the physical plane.

But we can, starting with the time when the child begins to babble, accustom it to pronounce the name of Jesus and offer it pictures referring to Christ. However, we will not feel a deeper understanding preparing itself in the heart of a child at the very beginning of life. One thing is clear to anyone who can look into the mind of a child with the means of spiritual science: the first time one can help even the feeblest feeling for Christ to dawn through outer pedagogical methods is when the child reaches the point in its life that it can later remember—when its consciousness of its "I" awakens. Certainly no great understanding will be present in the first years after consciousness of the "I" awakens, but any kind representation that has something of the life of the Christ impulse in its words and pictures, and that we communicate without dogma will benefit, for the rest of his or her life, the person this child will become.

After the awakening of consciousness of the "I," we can indeed do some things, even when only a dim consciousness is present. For example, a child looks at the Sistine Madonna and Christ on the cross entirely differently after the awakening of consciousness of the "I" than before, even though we cannot yet begin to make an effect on that child through physical means.

The Mystery of Golgotha entered the earthly development of humanity and is destined to have its effect on the progress of spiritual life on the physical plane. And a human being actually first really sets foot onto the physical plane consciously when the "I" awakens. But what is there before this?

Three things precede the awakening of the "I" in the child. I have already alluded to these in earlier lectures—they are things of enormous importance. The child learns to walk, which means it learns to raise itself up out of the position from which it was incapable of directing its bodily stance away from the Earth to the heavenly heights of the universe. It learns to bring itself out of the horizontal position into the vertical position.

By this, human beings primarily distinguish themselves from beasts. Through its own inner power, the child learns to assume an upright posture and to turn its gaze away from the earthly. The animal, through its entire determined nature and form, must necessarily have its gaze directed to the earthly. The exceptions to this are only seeming ones. The child learns the upright posture before consciousness of the "I" awakens. We actually recapitulate in our present post-Atlantean life all the things we as human beings have appropriated in the course of time. What we made our own only gradually during the ancient Lemurian age—learning to walk and stand upright—we now repeat in childhood before our "I" consciously awakens. This learning is compressed into the time when it does not yet depend upon our consciousness. It still functions as an unconscious impulse. Animals that have an approximately vertical, approximately upward-pointing gait have their entire organism so organized that they naturally assume this position, which is, in fact, fundamentally not entirely erect. It would be a false comparison if animals that become approximately vertical were considered to be like human beings.

A human being is called in the first period of life—before consciousness of the "I" awakens, yet through the disposition of the "I"—to bring itself into an upright, vertical posture, to raise itself out of the position in which it existed in the ancient Moon age. The direction of its backbone was then parallel to the surface of the Moon. It was primarily horizontal. In the ancient Lemuria, human beings learned to transform the Moon orientation into an earthly orientation. This arose because, out of their own substance, the spirits of form[†] first instilled the "I" into the human being during the development of the Earth.

The first manifestation of this influx of the "I" is the inner power through which the human being straightens up and is thereby, as it were, snatched away from the Earth. The Earth itself has inner spiritual forces that can flow through the backbone if it remains horizontal in its natural growth, as in the body of an animal. But the Earth has no power within itself to serve the human being directly. The human being can stand upright because of the "I." Later the consciousness of the 'I" will awaken so that the human being can develop harmoniously in its upright, vertical gait. Forces must flow in from out of the cosmos. However, because the human being was torn away from the spiritual powers of the Earth, Lucifer and Ahriman would have been able to bring human development into disorder—if the first Christ event had not intervened during the ancient Lemurian period.

During this ancient Lemurian period, in the spiritual realm closest to our earthly realm, the Christ being interpenetrated the being that later became the Nathan Jesus, who then, however, was a kind of angelic being. That was a preliminary stage to the Mystery of Golgotha. The consequence was that during ancient Lemuria—in the etheric spiritual heights, however—the future Nathan Jesus, who otherwise would have had the form of an angel, assumed an etheric human form, naturally not a fleshly one. In the closest region above the Earth, Jesus of Nazareth was to be found as an etheric angel form. Through its suffusion with the Christ being, the future Nathan Jesus then assumed etheric human form. With that, something new entered into the cosmos. This then radiated forth over the Earth and made it possible for the physical form of the earthly human being, into which the power of the etheric Christ being flowed, to protect itself from the destruction that would have forced its way in, if the formative power that makes it a proper, upright being had not been able to shine into, interpenetrate, and live within it. If the formative power, which is able to shine in because the first Christ event took place, had not flowed in with the physical Sun forces, chaos would necessarily have come. What the human received through this has been living in the evolution of humanity since ancient Lemuria.

We are looking at a developing human child in the right way if we recognize that when the child straightens itself up from a creeping, crawling, helpless state and stands or walks for the first time, this can only happen properly and for the benefit of humankind because, in the ancient Lemurian age, the first Christ event took place and the spiritual etheric being who was the Nathan Jesus took on human etheric form through being permeated by the Christ.

Truly, spiritual science exists so that we may enrich our feelings. Such feelings as can live in our souls when we see a child standing up and learning to walk certainly have a deep religious background. We should remember why a child walks, and then think how the Christ impulse is to be thanked for it. Thus we enrich our worldview through spiritual science and gain a feeling that we could not otherwise have for what surrounds us. We notice, at the same time through spiritual science, the protector or guardian of a child's growth and development. We notice how the Christ force radiates all around the being and growth of the child.

In my presentation from the akashic chronicle for the Lemurian period,[†] which discusses our Lemurian ancestors, you will see that these ancestors were mute. The Atlantean human first really learned to speak. How this happened is explained in those essays on the akashic chronicle. Learning to speak is the second of the abilities the child appropriates before true consciousness of the "I" awakens. The awakening of the consciousness of the "I" follows learning to speak. Learning to speak rests entirely on a sort of imitation, whose foundations lie deep in human nature.

Speaking is a second human ability that entered earthly humanity through its evolutionary course of development. Because the spirits of form poured through human beings, interpenetrating them, we are able to speak a language and to live our earthly lives on the physical plane. Thus through a second element, language, we tear ourselves away from the Earth, from the spiritual forces that are active within the Earth. Animals are suffused with these spiritual forces of the Earth and do not really learn to speak. Even speaking with gestures of the animal is not the same as human speech. If through training or some other means we were to make a speech possible for the animal that was similar to human beings, conditions would arise outside its body that would have to be discussed by spiritual science, but are outside our topic today. We want to stay with the normal development of the human being.

The disposition for human speech was given through what the spirits of form poured in from divine heights. Let us stop here and observe how human beings transformed themselves from muteness into speaking beings. They freed themselves from the forces that wash through the Earth spiritually, just as they freed themselves from the first stream by standing upright. Through the influence of Lucifer and Ahriman, everything connected with speech would have become base if human beings had been left entirely to the ministrations of Earth, if cosmic-spiritual influences that came down to Earth had not poured themselves into the human being. Without these cosmic influences, humanity would not have properly developed its entire life culture, all its physical organs—the larynx, tongue, throat, and so forth, and indeed even the deeper-lying organs, like the heart and so on, insofar as they relate to speech. If nothing had happened through Christ, during the Atlantean period, human beings would have developed their organs in such a way that they would have been capable of expressing themselves only in a meager babble—like a sibyl or a medium—about what causes them egotistical pain, joy, desire, or passion. Human beings would be able to produce far more artistic sounds than an animal, but their sounds would have been expressions only for what lives inside them. They would have living interjections or feeling words to express physical processes taking place in the organism. The whole of language would consist only of interjections. While now we keep the number of interjections in our languages to a minimum, without the intervention of Christ, the human art of speaking in its full complexity would have developed only to the point of interjections. This was averted in human evolution. The second Christ event averted the disorder in the power of speech that meant one could express only what was interior. This happened through the fact that, in the etheric heights, the being who later became the Nathan Jesus was imbued a second time with the Christ being and assumed an essence that so penetrated human physical organs that, from then on, human beings became capable of uttering something other than interjections. The second Christ event made human beings capable of grasping what is objective.

Yet, language, the power of speech, the human ability to express the movements of the soul in words, was still in danger. Through the second Christ event it could well have happened that human beings would not only have found sounds, interjections or feeling words for what lay within them, but also in a certain way could have loosened the inner movement of speech. However, indicating external things through words so that words can be correct signs for external things still remained endangered by luciferic and ahrimanic influences well into the Atlantean period.

Then came the third Christ event. For the third time the being in the spiritual heights, who was later born as the Nathan Jesus, united with the Christ being and once again poured itself, with the forces it assumed at that time, into the human capability of speech. The power of this Christ Jesus Being now penetrated for a second time the organs in the human body having to do with the power of speech. This penetration gave the power of speech the possibility to craft words that are real signs for external surroundings, and thereby crafted language as a means of communication throughout the individual regions of humanity.

The child could never learn to speak if these two Christ events had not occurred in the Atlantean age. Once again we enrich our feeling through spiritual science if, when the child begins to speak and perfects its speaking, we then think about how the Christ impulses rule within the unconscious and how the power of Christ lives in the power of speech as protector and helper.

After the three Christ events, which I have discussed again today from a certain point of view regarding their influence on human development, there came the post-Atlantean period.

In post-Atlantean development, first the peoples of the Egypto-Chaldean culture have the task of repeating what happened for humanity during ancient Lemuria, but penetrating it with consciousness. Utterly unconsciously, human beings learned to be upright beings in the Lemurian age and to be speaking beings in the Atlantean age. Human beings had received the Christ impulse into themselves quite unconsciously because their power of thinking had not yet been awakened.

In the post-Atlantean age, they were to be led slowly to understand what they had received unconsciously in ancient times. It was the Christ impulse that allowed human beings to stand upright and to look upward to the cosmic heights. Human beings at first experienced this Christ impulse unconsciously as it was experienced in the Lemurian age. Then, not yet fully conscious, but as if in a state of preparation for full consciousness, the peoples of Egypt were guided to revere what lives in the human power of raising oneself upright. The initiates of Egyptian culture made sure that the people learned to revere the power of becoming vertical by making them erect the pyramids, which rise up from the Earth to the heavens. We must still admire today how, through the intervention of cosmic powers, this uprightness was brought to expression in the entire form and position of the pyramid structure. The obelisks were erected there, so that the human beings would begin to penetrate what the power of uprightness is. The wonderful hieroglyphs in the pyramids and on the obelisks, which were supposed to point to the Christ, awakened the spiritual powers from the Lemurian age.

Although the Egyptians were able to arrive at a dim understanding of the power of uprightness, they were incapable in respect to the power of speech. Their mind had first to achieve the proper training in feeling so that human beings in later times could understand the riddle of how Christ lives in the human gift for words. This riddle was to be taken up by the maturing human soul with the most devout awe. The hierophants, the initiates of Egyptian culture, took care of this in a wonderful way by erecting the enigmatic sphinx with its mute, adamant form, which resonated under the influence of the cosmos mainly for the exaltation of the people of that time. In looking at the mute sphinx, which began to resound from out of the cosmos through the rising Sun under certain conditions and relationships, the deep reverence of the soul took form. Through this awe, the soul was prepared to understand the speech that must be spoken in the time when it was to be brought to higher consciousness. In what the sphinx could not yet say, it laid the groundwork for what was to be said to humanity. The impulse of Christ lies in the forming of the movement of the word. This was said to humanity in the words:

In the beginning was the Word,
And the Word was with God,
And the Word was a God.
This was in the beginning with God.
There it was, where everything came into being,
And nothing came into being
Except through the Word.
In the Word was life,
And life was
The light of human beings.

"In the Word was life, and life was the light of human beings"—this Word stands at the place where the Gospel was born from the fourth post-Atlantean period, when, prepared by Greco-Roman culture, people had arrived at the point of recapitulating in the fourth post-Atlantean cultural period what had transpired in the Atlantean age. Just as the veneration of uprightness was recapitulated in the Egyptian age, so now the veneration of the Word was recapitulated. In this way, superhuman spiritual forces work their way into the development of humanity.

The third thing the child must learn, before really awakening to consciousness of the "I," is representation or thinking. Thinking in this sense was reserved for the humanity of the post-Atlantean age; basically it came, in fact, first for the people of the fourth post-Atlantean period. Before that time, human beings thought in images. I will speak of this in my forthcoming book *The Riddles of Philosophy*. A child, in fact, thinks in images. Thinking thoughts was first given to humanity, was first awakened, in the six and seventh centuries before Christ. Since then, thinking thoughts continued to develop ever further. We are standing now in the midst of this unfolding. Such thinking of thoughts evolves in such a way that it seizes our "I." The fourth Christ event, the Mystery of Golgotha, took place so that such thinking may also be connected to the Christ impulse, and not lapse into disorder in its effect on the "I." And if our thinking is to become increasingly ordered and continue to develop so that thoughts do not become chaotic and confusing, but rather are permeated with inner feeling so that a healthy truth-thinking should continue to develop, this will all happen because thinking has been able to attain the impulse to do so through the Mystery of Golgotha. Such thinking will take place because of the fourth Christ event, when the Christ impulse poured itself out into the spiritual atmosphere of the Earth.

The pouring forth of the Christ impulse happened for the first time in the Lemuria, when Lucifer threatened the upright nature of the human being. It happened a second time in the Atlantean age, when human beings were snatched away from the danger that threatened their speech through the fact that speech is expression from within outward. There was a danger of speech lapsing into disorder. Towards the end of the Atlantean age, a third intervention occurred through Christ's interpenetration of the being, who later became Jesus of Nazareth. Through this act, the gift of speech, insofar as it became a sign for external things, was saved from danger.

The fourth danger[†] concerned thinking, the inner representation of thoughts. Human beings are saved from this danger through penetrating with their thoughts such forms as that which has flowed out through the Mystery of Golgotha into the spiritual sphere of the Earth and which can live within us, if we are willing and have prepared ourselves through spiritual science.

We are far enough along in the development of humanity that the first words of the Gospel of John may be expressed in another form:

> In the beginning is the thought,
> And the thought is with God,
> And a divine thing is the thought,
> In it there is life,
> And life should become the light of my "I."
> And may the divine thought shine in my "I,"
> So that the darkness of my "I" may grasp
> The divine thought.

Although it was not understood fully, such was the direction in the development of humanity.

The fourth post-Atlantean culture began in the eighth century of the pre-Christian age. About three and a half centuries later, thinking was sufficiently mature that it could be expressed by the Greek philosophers with the clarity that led to Platonic philosophy. Then human life was penetrated with the Christ impulse. The fifth post-Atlantean period began with the fifteenth century after Christ. The time from the beginning of the fourth post-Atlantean period to the understanding of thought is exactly as long as the time from the beginning of the fifth post-Atlantean period to a conscious expression of the nature of thinking, that is, until Hegel. Human thinking experienced its peak in Hegel with the statement, "The life and activity of thinking in truth is spirit at work." What Hegel said in such an apparently incomprehensible way can be expressed with the words:

> In the beginning was the thought,
> And unending is the thought,
> And the life of thought is the light of the "I."
> May radiant thought fill
> The darkness of my "I,"
> So that the darkness of my "I" may comprehend it,
> The living thought,
> And live and weave in its divine beginning.

The development of humanity proceeds in this way. Humanity has not come very far precisely because Hegel has been maligned a great deal. One could truly say: "And radiant thinking appeared in the darkness, but the darkness wanted no part of it." If we learn to understand our life, the life of thinking, then we will understand what will be incumbent upon humanity in its more distant existence.

At the same time, because we work from the basis of spiritual science, there is still something more. Later epochs are always prepared in earlier epochs. While we are cultivating spiritual science in the midst of the fifth post-Atlantean period and have more and more to contribute to the understanding of living thinking, thinking that is becoming clairvoyant, we have at the same time to prepare for the sixth post-Atlantean period.

Life flows into thoughts through the Christ impulse. The Christ impulse will also flow into something that belongs to the capacities of the human soul and should not be confused with thinking alone. The child develops its capabilities out of the unconscious. In that it attains consciousness of the "I," it enters the sphere where it can appropriate and must develop what, through the Christ impulse, can come in from without. As the child learns to walk and to speak and begins to work its way through to the "I" by learning to think, we can gradually see how the conscious Christ impulse, which entered through the Mystery of Golgotha, has its effect on children.

There is something else that lies in the faculties of the soul into which humanity today cannot yet receive the Christ impulse. Leading this Christ impulse into upright walking, into speaking, and into thinking† is possible through what has existed within human culture for centuries. If we base ourselves on spiritual science in the right way, we must think about bringing the Christ impulse into a fourth element and about preparing this introduction into a fourth human faculty. We must bear this in mind!

Where the Christ impulse cannot yet be led, but is being prepared to be led, is into *human memory*. For, beyond walking and standing upright, speaking, and thinking, the power of Christ is now entering memory. We can understand the Christ when he speaks to us through the Gospels. However, we human beings are being prepared for Christ to enter into thoughts, which then live on within us as remembered thoughts and representations. And a time will arrive for humanity in the sixth greater period of human development—but it is now being prepared—when people will look at what they have experienced, which lives in them as memory, and will see that Christ lives with them in the power of memory. Christ will be able to speak through every memory picture. Moreover, when we give new life to the representations that are so connected with us in our memory, Christ will be present in the memory. We will be able to look back at our lives and recognize that, just as we remember, just as the power of remembrance lives in us, so also the Christ impulse, which has been poured into that power, lives in this remembrance. The way that has been ordered for human beings to make more and more true the words, "Not I, but Christ in me," will be made smooth by the fact that the Christ impulse will gradually take up residence in the power of memory. The Christ impulse is not yet within memory. When the Christ impulse will not only live in the human intellect, but will also pour itself out over the whole tract of memories, then human beings will not be wholly dependent on external documents to learn history, for the power of recollection will expand. Christ will live in this memory.

And because Christ will live in the human power of memory, human beings will know how he worked from beyond the Earth up until the Mystery of Golgotha, how he prepared and underwent this Mystery of Golgotha, and how he continues to work further as an impulse in history. We will have this overview just as we have memory today. We will not be able to survey the earthly development of humanity without seeing the Christ impulse at its center. All power of recollection will be penetrated by the Christ impulse and at the same time be strengthened through that penetration. For those of us who are to comprehend Christianity in a living way, also these words can be valid in the future:

> In the beginning is memory,
> And memory lives on,
> And divine is memory,
> And memory is life,
> And this life is the "I" of human beings,
> Which flows in human beings themselves.
> Not they alone, but Christ in them.
> When they remember divine life
> There in their memory is the Christ,
> And as radiant memory-life
> The Christ will shine
> In every immediately present darkness.

We will be able to say: "Christ is in the inner life of our soul." Many of us will feel this, because we will learn to connect ourselves with the Christ impulse through memory, just as we learned as children to straighten ourselves up, to speak, because we connected with the Christ impulse. Many of us also feel that because our current capacity of remembrance is in a preparatory state, it would, in the future, lapse into disorder if it did not have the will to let itself be permeated with the Christ impulse. If materialism on Earth were to deny the Christ, then memory would come into disorder. Then, more and more people would appear whose memory would become chaotic and who would become duller and duller in their dark "I" consciousness because memory did not shine into this dusky consciousness of the "I." Our powers of remembrance can only develop properly if the Christ impulse is viewed correctly. Then history will live like a living memory, so that the understanding for true events enters into memory. Then human memory will understand the midpoint of world events. Then vision will become valid for human beings. Common memory, which focuses only on one life, will extend itself over previous incarnations. Remembrance is now a process of preparation that will be completed through Christ. Whether we look outward at how we developed unconsciously as children, or whether we turn our gaze within, or, through extensive deepening of our inner selves, look as far as what remains as our inner self in memory, we see the living power and activity of the Christ impulse everywhere.

The new Christ event, which is now approaching, not physically but etherically, is connected with the first kindling of the ability to remember, with the first unfolding of the suffusion of memory with Christ. In this penetrating of memory, Christ will approach human beings as an angelic being. We must prepare ourselves for that. Hence spiritual science should not enrich us merely with theories, but should pour into us something that makes us capable of receiving what confronts us in the world, and what we ourselves are, with other feelings. Our life of feelings and sensations can be enriched, if we penetrate with spiritual science in the right way into the essence of the Christ impulse and its workings in the human being and in the spiritual nature of the human being. It is good to often think the following:

> In the beginning was the force of memory.
> The force of memory shall become divine,
> And a divine thing shall the force of memory become.
> Everything that arises in the "I"
> Shall become such
> That it is a creation from memory imbued with Christ,
> with the Divine.
> In it there shall be life,

And in it there shall be radiant light,
Which from thought that remembers
Shines into the darkness of the present.
And may darkness, as it is at present,
Comprehend the light of memory become divine.

If we take in the sense of such words, then we receive something that is right for human beings to acquire. As the plant forms the seed for the life of the next plant, we learn not only to sense within ourselves the fruits that come to us from earlier incarnations, but also to sense, so that we understand how to pass over into following incarnations. In following incarnations our capabilities of memory would be in a very sorry state if we did not imbue ourselves with the Christ impulse. Thinking is still only minimally interpenetrated with the Christ impulse and it is already approaching the memory. Let us learn from spiritual science to live not only for what is temporal in human beings, but for that which is eternal in human beings, for that which passes through repeated incarnations. And let us learn through spiritual science what the right understanding and the right feeling for the strongest impulse in the whole evolution of humanity—the Christ impulse—can mean for the full realization of our own soul life.

8

The Christ Spirit and Its Relation to the Evolution of Consciousness

MUNICH, MARCH 30, 1914†

EVERYTHING that enters our efforts is crystallized in the end around one point: finding the connection with the spiritual powers that carry humanity forward. From this point of view, again and again the topic here has been the significance of the Christ being in the world. Today I should like to say a few words that should be suitable to make our ideas about the Christ impulse and its relationship with us human beings increasingly more substantial. If we wish to grasp the Christ impulse in its reality, we must get used to reflecting on various things. Indeed, in our time we hear nothing more than the thought expressed here and there that one should repress everything smacking of the schoolmaster, everything pedantic, everything didactic, and seize on living life in art and philosophy. So many minds of the present express their fatigue with everything academic. It is remarkable that just as philosophical issues become the topic, one falls back again and again into the yearning for the academic.

We have had to listen to people speaking about Christ as though about a world teacher. I once used the expression "superhuman schoolmaster to the world." Many people feel good when they can think that with Christ someone came into the world who taught something. In contrast, we have repeatedly stressed the character of the life and the character of the power of the Christ impulse. Through what happened at the baptism in the Jordan, a being found the way into earthly life through sharing the fate of humanity for three years. Then this being flowed out into the aura of the Earth and since then carries on its work there.

If one looks at the Christ event, one must say that this event of Golgotha is a unique experience in the evolution of the Earth. It was accomplished once in the evolution of the Earth; however, the Christ event was prepared in the spiritual world. Although it is thoroughly false to think of the Christ being as being in another body, one must nonetheless refer to a preparatory event, or namely, three preliminary stages to the event of Golgatha in the evolution of the world. They transpired in the purely spiritual worlds.

I spoke about the two boys named Jesus, the Solomon Jesus boy and the Nathan Jesus boy. The Solomon boy carried the "I" of Zoroaster, which then went over into the other boy and lived there from the twelfth to the thirtieth year. Then the "husk", the sheath of this Jesus was filled with the Christ being. This Nathan Jesus was also thus properly incarnated in a human body in the world for the first time. (That must be expressly mentioned.) He was born at the beginning of our time reckoning, and previous to that, he was never actually incarnated in a human body. The relation to Krishna was not an actual incarnation, but an ersatz incarnation.† If we consider the essence of this later Nathan Jesus, we must look to the angelic being and say that he was not incarnated before Christ appeared on the Earth, but rather was present in the spiritual world and was ensouled three times. And in each of these three stages of existence something similar to the event of Golgotha occurred for him. We must therefore seek in the spiritual worlds the stages that presaged Golgotha. Each of these events has a deep significance for the entire life of human beings on Earth. What we there experience is not influenced only by what happens within the physical world, but also from spiritual worlds. The effects of the three preliminary stages were brought in from outside the earthly realm.

The luciferic influence had already descended over humanity in the Lemurian epoch. Lucifer sent, as it were, his rays of power into human nature, affecting it inwardly. The human being would have necessarily developed in another way if no luciferic influence had come. The human being was, so to speak, infected with the luciferic impulse. From the viewpoint of spiritual science, we can say what the effect of this luciferic influence was. Had this influence remained as strong as in Lemuria, something would have gravely threatened our human nature. We can characterize what would have occurred approximately like this: The twelve powers of the human senses—for there are twelve†—would have formed in such a way that the human being would have become oversensitive. The red of the rose has an objective effect on us today as we look at it; at that time red would have pierced our eyes as if with barbs, and blue would have sucked on our power of sight. We would have been oversensitive. It would have been the same with hearing and the other human sense impressions. We would have been able to perceive nothing without feeling pain or desire. That was what confronted humanity through Lucifer.

The beings of the upper hierarchies saw this. The Nathan Jesus who lived on Earth at a later time was present as an angelic being in the spiritual world during the Lemurian age, and his task was to be penetrated by the Christ being. While the sheaths were later penetrated with the Christ being, the soul elements of this angelic being were spiritually imbued with the Christ impulse. Already back then, the Christ impulse sank down into the soul of the future Nathan Jesus. This event occurred in the spiritual world, but the radiance emerging from it spread out over the Earth and soothed the oversensitive human senses, so that the danger that people could only behold the sense world with either pain or debasing lust was eliminated. So we look at the first harbinger of the event of Golgotha and recognize that our twelve senses became as they are, due to the fact that the Christ sank into the soul of the future Nathan Jesus and softened the nature of the human senses.

Then, in the Atlantean age, a danger once again came into human life through a gradual joining together of the ahrimanic influence with the luciferic influence. While in Lemuria it was the senses that confronted a danger, now in the early Atlantean period, the life organs and the etheric body of the human being stood in danger. Had these organs of the etheric body been permeated with the influence of Lucifer and Ahriman, human beings would have assumed a form unworthy of the human being. Everything would have been made in such a way that human beings would have pursued what was useful to them with avidity, and could only have looked at what was not advantageous with disgust. Human life would have run its course between greed and repulsion. All organs would have been so constituted that human beings would have pounced in a degrading fashion like a wild animal on what they had to take, and, would have felt deeply humiliated if confronted by anything that was not beneficial to them. That this did not come to pass was due to the second preliminary stage of the event of Golgotha. The danger was such that even in breathing, human beings would have sucked in the air with greed, and every glimmer of something unsuited to them would have been met with terrible outbursts of repulsion. This was the second time this angelic being was permeated with the Christ impulse, and through that, rays of power entered the aura of the Earth and softened the life of human beings.

Toward the end of the Atlantean period, the third preliminary stage developed. Again humanity confronted a great danger. Now thinking, feeling, and willing were about to become chaotic. The expressions of the soul were about to be thrown out of harmony, so that human beings would not have been able to develop thinking, feeling, and willing in an orderly way; rather, these would have rushed around and through one another as if mad. This disharmony was deflected by the third preliminary stage. Once again the being who later became the Nathan Jesus was penetrated with the Christ impulse, and order and harmony was introduced to the attunement of thinking, feeling, and willing. This was still felt for a long time in post-Atlantean times. In times that preceded our development of thinking, the harbingers of an image that reaches into our time, but is not yet rightly understood, already took form. At the end of the Atlantean age, Christ interpenetrated this soul that later became Jesus of Nazareth, with the result that this being became the eternal lord of these effects that wildly stormed around each other, became the victor over thinking, feeling, and willing, which were developing into excessively dense formations. Humanity represented this victory in the image of St. George or Michael, the dragon-slayer. That is the direct imaginative expression of the third forerunner of the event of Golgotha.

The Greeks, who brought to life in their imaginations what shone over from the secrets of Atlantis, created a divinity from the being that was active in Atlantis. They venerated in Apollo the spirit they imagined to be suffused with the Sun-Spirit. They did not name it Christ, but the name doesn't matter. In their Sun service they venerated the third preliminary stage of the event of Golgotha and expressed it outwardly when they took counsel of the priests of Apollo in the most weighty circumstances. These Greeks knew that interwoven in the secrets of existence is what weaves in the aura of the Earth, and they knew how it brought order to thinking, feeling, and willing. They felt that this event was so connected with the Earth, that they said that what climbed up in a dense form from the Earth, if it had not been conquered by Apollo, would have brought thinking, feeling, and willing into disorder. But Apollo brings in order, so that instead of dissonance or madness, wisdom flows from the aura of the Earth into thinking, feeling, and willing.

The Greeks looked for the place where steam gushed forth from the earth, which they stopped up and caught up in their temple, in order to place the priestess of Apollo over the opening. Apollo spoke through the priestess so that she changed into an oracle, giving advice for the situations of those seeking this wisdom. As George and Michael appear in the images, so it is with Apollo in his sanctuary, pouring the prophecies speaking though him into the soul.

Oh, Christianity is very ancient! The name of Christ doesn't matter. The worship of Apollo venerated Christ, the Sun-Spirit, so that in this veneration lies the consciousness of the third preliminary event of Golgotha.

Then the time came when humanity stood before a fourth great danger. In Lemuria the physical body was in danger, and then in Atlantis the etheric organs and the astral organs. Now it was the "I" that was about to lapse into disorder. In preparation for that, when the "I" was about to take hold of the human being in Greek thought life, a very strange phenomenon appeared in which all the conditions were present to bring disorder into the "I." People will only gradually understand how what was supposed to drive this "I" forth developed in Greek philosophy, and so on. I have already attempted to show how the "I" awakened. Through contemplating philosophy, which reaches its peak in the thought life of Plato and Aristotle, it becomes apparent how the "I" was gradually approaching. As Thales, Pherecydes of Syros, and Anaxagoras† were first calling the great ideas to life, a parallel phenomenon spread from Greece over the entire Greek world. Parallel to the approach of the "I" came the phenomenon of the Sibyls.

The Sibyls asserted themselves everywhere during this time, occasionally expressing great wisdom for the future, but also, in part, madness. Everything that can bring the "I" into disorder was expressed in their prophecies: the "I" must lapse into disorder without the Christ impulse. Two sorts of things were being prepared: on the one side the prophets, the preparers of the Christ impulse; they sought to receive the young Christ force in the deepening of the soul and experienced, in an ordered thought life, what weaves through the evolution of humanity. On the other side were the Sibyls, who were devoted to the external influences of the Earth's aura. We encounter this opposition of Sibyls and prophets in Michelangelo's representation in the Sistine Chapel in Rome. Michelangelo shows how the wind and what was connected with the elemental nature of Earth were at work among the Sibyls. Michelangelo shows that the danger of the "I" lapsing into disorder was present with the Sibyls, as well as how the prophets were at work to quiet the "I." Comparing the prophets with the Sibyls in Michelangelo's pictures can guide us deeply into many secrets. How the human "I" will lapse into disorder in the fourth stage is demonstrated in the powers of the Sibyls. The order proclaimed by the teaching of the prophets was fulfilled through the Mystery of Golgotha: the ordering of the "I" forces in the form that the human "I" learned to feel ever more deeply, "Not I, but Christ in me." What in the Sibyls would have necessarily contributed to the disorder of the "I" emerges in an orderly fashion through the Christ impulse. Because the "I" of human beings must develop on Earth, the event of Golgotha had to take place on Earth. Christ had to permeate the body of Jesus, the real physical body, while in the preliminary stages, an angel's soul was permeated.

Thus, Golgotha approached the development of the Earth. What Augustine said has deep truth: "Christianity has always been there; it is only that one calls it Christianity now."† In Augustine's times, one felt something of the fact that Apollo's worshippers were Christians, if not by name. People venerated the third preliminary event, which was still spiritual. In this way Christ gradually approached the Earth. The first and second stages were in devachan, the third in the astral world, and the event of Golgotha in the physical world.

However, Christ did not penetrate the aura of the Earth as a teacher, but with his power. That must be emphasized over and over again. If Christ had only wanted to do his work through what people could have understood from him, he would have been able to produce little result. He entered evolution as a living being. Human understanding must wrestle its way up to him. We see how disputes of dogma are played out in this struggle. Human judgment is still far from penetrating the Christ impulse, which works into the depths of the soul as a living force.

We can follow this force. Let us look at an event of October 28, 312. At that time Constantine fought a pitched battle with Maxentius outside of Rome. Maxentius's army was four times as strong as Constantine's, yet Constantine won. A person who observes history in the right way recognizes that the life of all of Europe would have been different, if Constantine had not won. It was a remarkable battle. Neither external strength nor judgment prevailed. The battle was not fought with what proceeded from judgment. It was fought from both sides with subconscious impulses, into which the Christ impulse played. Maxentius consulted the sibylline books, which told him: "If you do not stay in the place where you are, if you go out from Rome, you will enslave the great enemy of Rome." Also a dream told him he should leave Rome and fight before the gates. In Rome he was securely entrenched. Human judgment did not determine what was at play in this battle. The subconscious worked into the souls of Maxentius and Constantine. A dream revealed to Constantine that he should carry the symbol of Christianity at the head of his army. Dreams decided this battle, which determined the fate of Europe. Human judgment was not capable of bringing about what had to happen; rather the Christ impulse intervened and positioned the four-times-weaker army of Constantine to oppose Maxentius outside Rome. Human affairs were led through what human beings cannot judge. This is significant for the entire guidance of human history.

The Christ impulse made its effect in the subconscious of souls as a spiritual impulse. It worked in the same way later, when once again the map of Europe received a totally different form. If the Maid of Orleans had not come to the side of her king at the decisive moment, all the destinies of Europe would have been different. Once again it was not judgment, but the Christ impulse, which made use of a human instrument. It is not for us to judge whether one finds this good or bad.

I can show in another example, how the Christ impulse works under the threshold of consciousness. It avails itself of strange manifestations, strange to a materialist. As modern spiritual life approached, there was something in its development that would have caused materialism to stretch its arms over European life to an even greater extent. If certain processes had not appeared, it might have been possible that entirely material ideas would have entered even those souls that still felt themselves to be spiritual. Already in earlier centuries the understanding for the Christ impulse would have declined so far that people would have doubted his physical existence. In that case Arthur Drews and others would have had a much easier time of it.† A mood spread over the most distant parts of Europe in the sixteenth and seventeenth centuries, when the danger of losing the connection with the Christ impulse was at hand, that questioned why we should believe that Christ actually lived. And it came about that the same thing happened at the same time in the most diverse parts of Europe. In almost all the regions of Europe, everywhere, it turned out that a physical person, but always a different one in different areas, went through the most diverse human settlements, villages and cities. The opinion was circulated that this human personality, who appeared turned out in an especially peculiar way, was Ahasver, the eternal Jew, who has wandered through the world since he rejected Christ. The news spread that there was a living person who could say from personal observation, "I have seen Christ. He really lived." This person went, in a most dreadful state, in old, worn-out clothing, through villages in the most varied places. He took part in religious services and told the story of the event for which he could stand as a witness. Bishops and abbots invited such personages to banquets and organized festivities for them. These personalities always told the same story: "I can confirm for you from knowledge that Christ walked the Earth, for he passed by me, and because I dismissed him like that, I must now wander through the world in this way."

From what we learn from history, we have no idea how deeply Ahasver's story affected human minds a couple of centuries ago. There were always different individuals who saw, as if in a kind of an Ahasver-review or reflection, Christ pass by them; so people believed them. The consciousness arose: "Yes! He lived, because he can tell the story." Superficial people today can ask if that should have had such a great influence, as to avert the danger that Christ would be forgotten as a historical Christ. They don't know that such events happened in the world without history ever recording them. That we are today not totally bogged down in materialism is a result of what proceeded from these personalities. Today that could not happen. In certain places, Ahasver had thick calluses, peculiar clothing, long hair, yellowish skin and was tall and haggard; in other places he was short, and had a humpback—but always he had the awareness of being permeated by the sight which the soul believed it experienced in the moment Christ passed by in front of him.

This consciousness, this ability to look back into the akashic chronicle and to identify with it so strongly that they really believed it, had sunk into numerous personalities. Today all these Ahasvers would end up in the lunatic asylum; back then they were the instruments for the strengthening of spiritual life. Bishops and abbots themselves were strengthened through them in the power of belief in Christ. From spiritual worlds the seed of being able to look back to the event of Golgotha was planted in spiritually inclined natures. Through the peculiarity of their consciousness, the storytellers saw themselves as present in the picture. It was the true, living vision of the event of Golgotha. Much more than in the upper regions of human consciousness, in which the power of judgment is significant, what came from the Christ impulse played itself out in the subconscious regions of the soul. The materialistically minded human beings of today can easily scorn such things, considering it a psychic epidemic, and ask how we can rely on what comes from diseased souls. We might like to ask these materialists what they would say when a man so mentally ill that the psychiatrists lock him up in a lunatic asylum, but that he then begins to conceive, out of his illumination, of the airplane engine, which is actually an idea that people have in mind today. They would accept that from such a soul without asking whether it came from a diseased mind. That is no criterion, no argument, for whether a soul is ill or not. It is a matter of testing the content of what comes from the soul. The worst thing about our materialistic spirit is that one appeals to secondary considerations and not to the force of truth.

If we survey the evolution of humanity, it will become clear that we should understand the Christ impulse as a living force, which is much more active in the lower levels of the soul and avails itself of physical means more than people understand. If Christ had remained limited to the physical, his influence would never have gone very far. However, in our time the situation is beginning to change, so that eventually that must be active in us, which for the Greek was thinking, with which, in fact, the consciousness of the human "I" was born at the same time. How does this thinking work today? One does not need to prove it with spiritual science, but rather with philosophy. In the centuries before the founding of Christianity, beginning with Pherecydes and ending with Aristotle, thinking got its start in the evolution of the world. Thinking in pictures first began in Greek life. That prepared the true consciousness of the "I." Then comes the Christ impulse, which works together with what has emerged as the force of the "I."

In our time we see it in Hegelian thought. Little attention has been paid to it, but how Hegel wrestles with the thinking that wants to comprehend the entire world is an important phenomenon of humanity. Human beings are evolving in the world; they crown their evolution through the by filling the world with thinking. Thinking completes the world. Human beings recognize their surroundings through it. However, thinking can achieve two things. It can develop properly, which can be compared with the development of the seed to the blossom. But the seed can also serve for human nutrition, in which case it will be torn out of its regular, continuing flow. If it stays in its continuous flow, it develops into a new plant; predictably, life for the future comes from it. It is the same with human thinking. We can say that through it we make pictures for ourselves of our surroundings. However, the employment of such knowledge is like using seeds for nutriment. We drive thinking from its flow. If, however, it remains in its flow, then we let it live its own seed-life. We let it unfold in meditation and inspiration and let it develop itself into a new, fertile existence. That is the right flow of thinking. In the future, we will recognize that what we have regarded as knowledge of the world behaves like the grain that does not progress to the new grain, but rather is driven out into a totally different flow. But the knowledge we learn through knowledge of the higher worlds is the thinking, that is philosophically comprehended in freedom and that leads directly into spiritual life through meditation and concentration.

We stand at a point where it will be recognized that ordinary knowledge is to supersensible knowledge as a grain used for food is to a grain that progresses to a new grain. Inner knowledge of thinking is what the future must bring. Philosophy of the old style has been overcome, is played out. We will know that such knowledge must always be there, but must lead to an evolutionary tributary. And we will know that living thinking, which transforms itself through meditation and concentration, leads to spiritual knowledge of human nature and to knowledge of the spiritual worlds.

If we observe various kinds of phenomena in our spiritual life, there is much that is striking. Here we may well say or discuss the sort of thing that would be misunderstood in the outside world. Today a person who is regarded as a great philosophical mind basically limits his wisdom to talking over and over again about the same subject. He says: "Human beings should not stop with mere external knowledge. They must grasp the spirit." He says over and over again, in another version: "Human beings cannot stop with mere external knowledge. They must grasp the spiritual within themselves, must experience it within themselves. It may not be grasped merely in concepts; it must come alive." Such people are not saying what spirit is; they know nothing about it. That is the hallmark of Eucken's philosophy.[†] It does not lead to true knowledge of the spirit. When we form thinking out of itself, it does not become a vague experience of spirit, but becomes whole in itself, and what we have learned to know as the etheric body comes toward it. In other words, if we transform thinking in meditation, our meditative thought will form itself. And then, out of the etheric body, our spiritual being will become present. Humanity is on its way in its evolution from philosophy to a living spiritual knowledge.

We are on the straight path. Those who see this understand their time, but it is not possible to gain a real insight into these things without developing reverence for the knowledge, which holds one back with the power of judgment that one has from applying the criterion universally. One must be willing to prepare oneself ever and again for new knowledge, for in its present state, the soul is suited only for a tributary of knowledge. Only when the soul develops to a higher level is it really suited to enter into the spiritual world. We first correctly understand our task within our community when we feel, with deep humility, how we are called to know something of this great change in all concepts of knowledge, which is intended to lead us into the spiritual world. We want to remain utterly modest, but because that is not a derogatory criticism, we can call many a person, who is recognized today as a great intellect, a shallow chatterer. We must find our way to unite humility with clear, strong, energetic judgment about what we are striving for and to know that we are actually standing only at the beginning. But our hearts can swell and glow with joy at the thought of what will come, of that toward which we are steering and to which we wish to devote the most intimate forces of our soul. I should like to turn not only to your power of imagination, but also to the deepest forces of your hearts, to that part of your souls where your deepest feeling for the pulse of the time is to be found. Then you will understand that such talk as this can only hint at what the leading powers of our time want to communicate to us, the spiritual individualities that we know are going through our stream of time. We will make no progress by acquiring only more and more concepts for what the spiritual world is. We must acquire them, but we only start to make real progress when we join with each new thought something that comes from the deepest foundation of our soul, so that this process of "understanding more and more" can prove itself before the leading powers of our time. We can feel them, how they speak in the most intimate foundation of our soul. Long before we hear this speaking as a warning, we can feel how our Anthroposophical Movement is carried by these spiritual leading powers, whose heralds we rightly are within our Movement. This consciousness should pour itself out over what we are doing as a true current of the soul.

9

Progress in the Knowledge of Christ: The Fifth Gospel

PARIS, MAY 27, 1914

In today's discussion† I should like to speak first about what we can now know about the Christ being from esoteric research, and then connect it to a discussion about the advances we have been able to make in the knowledge of Christ since the Mystery of Golgotha.

The great significance of the Mystery of Golgotha for the entire evolution of the Earth has been pointed out repeatedly within our spiritual movement. If the significance of the Mystery of Golgotha is pursued further within occult research, one finds three preliminary stages of the Mystery of Golgotha, which took place within the evolution of the Earth, and in connection with it. Three preliminary stages precede the Mystery of Golgotha and prepare it, but they were not played out on the physical plane; rather they were played out in the higher worlds.

The first of these events falls in the time of the Lemurian development of the world. The second and the third events fall in the time of the Atlantean development of the Earth. And the fourth is the Mystery of Golgotha, which took place on the physical plane in the post-Atlantean time, at the beginning of our time reckoning.

In the Lemurian time, the same being that we know as the Christ being united itself with another being of the higher worlds, which did not incarnate on the physical plane, but rather belonged to the world of the upper hierarchies. And so, as we can speak of Christ incarnating in the body of Jesus of Nazareth in relation to the Mystery of Golgotha, so can we speak about Christ taking up residence in an archangelic being of the higher worlds in the Lemurian age. We could say that an event similar to the later baptism by John on the physical plane transpired in the spiritual world during the Lemurian development. We meet therefore, in that ancient time, the Christ being in the soul body of an archangel. And through this sacrifice of the Christ being, its entry into the soul body of an archangel, a very particular effect was radiated into the development of the Earth.

In order to become familiar with the significance of this event, we must speak about a danger that stood before all human development in the Lemurian time through the forces of Lucifer. If this danger had not been deflected, everything we call the human faculties of sense perception would have come into disorder. The senses would not have developed under luciferic influence as they have developed; instead they would have become much more sensitive, much more excitable in relation to the external world. For example, it would then have been necessary for human beings to go through the world like this: if we had seen a blue color, it would have, so to speak, sucked at our eyes and we would have experienced something like a sucking force; and if we had seen the color red, we would have felt something like a piercing in the eyes. We must only imagine what we human beings would have become if, at every step in our lives, we were tossed about by nothing but exciting impressions through our sense perceptions. This danger was warded off because Christ ensouled himself in an archangelic being (I must say he did not incarnate), and the forces that therefore could shine out from the spiritual worlds poured themselves into the development of humanity, harmonizing the powers of the senses so that the danger was deflected and human beings obtained the necessary balance. Therefore, when we think today about how moderately our sense perceptions take their course, we can look back into the ancient Lemurian age and recognize that the sacrifice of Christ in ensouling himself in an archangelic being saved us from the danger of the hypersensitivity of our sense system.

In the beginning of the Atlantean period, the second danger threatened human development, now through Lucifer and Ahriman together.

This time the threat was an abnormal development of the life forces. These forces were about to develop in such a way that, for example, a hungry person would have pounced on food with bestial greed. On the other hand, any kind of food that was not good for people would have filled them with terrible disgust, and they would have fled from it. Hypersensitivity of the life forces threatened the human being at that time. Christ ensouled himself anew in an archangelic being of the upper hierarchies, and through this sacrifice the danger just described was warded off from humanity and the life forces were brought into harmony in such a way that we can now use them in moderation and balance.

The third danger threatened human development toward the end of the Atlantean age. The three soul forces, thinking, feeling, and willing, were about to lapse into disarray, and if this danger had not been deflected they would have had a disorderly, confused, chaotic effect.

If we want to understand the actual situation of this matter, we must understand clearly that the Earth is not only what the geologists think it is, a mineral body; rather that the Earth is an entire organism. What rises as foggy mist out of the ground of the Earth is not only a physical mist, but also the embodiment of passions, with luciferic and ahrimanic forces, which can unite with the passions and instincts of human beings. In the time stated, these would have caused chaos in the thinking, feeling, and willing of the human soul, and if this danger had not been deflected, the entire human race would have lapsed into a sort of delirium. The human race would have developed a state of madness, which would have become the normal condition of the Earth. At that point the Christ being ensouled himself in an archangelic being for the third time and warded off this danger through what could be once again be radiated into the development of humanity from this sacrifice. The effect of this third ensoulment of the Christ being is the harmonizing of thinking, feeling, and willing in the nature of the human soul.

The Greeks, who sensed something like afterimages of the processes during the Atlantean age, expressed the supersensible fact I have just described in their mythology. And the image, the afterimage, in which the Greeks represented the third ensoulment of Christ in an archangelic being, is Apollo the Sun god. Apollo, as the protector of the Pythia's pronouncements, appears as the being who harmonizes the dragon, which rises up out of the earth in the form of steam. If this mist had flowed into the passion of Pythia without Apollo's harmonization, thinking, feeling, and willing would have been expressed as madness. Through impregnation with the powers of Apollo, the Pythia's sayings became some of the wisest counsels given to the Greeks.

If one had been able to ask initiates in the ancient mysteries for their honest opinion of who Apollo was, they would most certainly have answered: "He is the precursor of Christ Jesus, who has not yet descended to the physical plane."

Humanity has received a wonderful imagination of this third Christ event in the picture *St. George Defeats the Dragon*, or *The Archangel Michael Defeats the Dragon*. It is wonderful to be able to be attentive to how this imagination of St. George defeating the dragon is a reverberation of the third supersensible Christ event.

And the fourth event came in the post-Atlantean time, when once again in the course of evolution, humanity was exposed to the danger of lapsing into disorder with respect to the forces of the soul. Now the human "I" itself was headed into disorder. The first danger consisted in the forces of the senses lapsing into disorder; the second danger in the life forces lapsing into disorder; the third danger in the soul forces, thinking, feeling, and willing, lapsing into disorder; the fourth danger in the forces of the "I" lapsing into disorder. The same being that had ensouled himself in a being three times before, the Christ being, now incarnated in Jesus of Nazareth in the Mystery of Golgotha to ward off this fourth danger from humanity through his radiating into the Earth's aura.

In the development of humanity in the centuries preceding and following the Mystery of Golgotha, we can see how the danger that was about to bring the "I" and its power into disorder was present. In Greek philosophy, in Socrates, Plato and Aristotle (already begun by Thales and Heraclitus), we can observe the blossoming of the forces of the "I," and we see also how something else makes its appearance alongside that blossoming. As the power of human thinking in Thales, Heraclitus, in Socrates, Plato, and Aristotle, blossomed, we see spreading over the entire civilized part of the Earth at approximately the same time, the powers of the so-called Sibyls showing themselves here and there. These

Sibyls, appearing as a parallel phenomenon beside the emergence of philosophy, make clear how chaos was about to penetrate the forces of the "I." On the one hand, we see how what these Sibyls proclaimed was true, soundly prophetic, and, on the other hand, we see misunderstandings, deceptive, disordered "I" forces speaking through them.

Michelangelo, drawing on tradition at a later date, shows wonderfully in the Sistine Chapel how the chaotic and earthly speaks out of the Sibyls. Right into the representation of the gestures we can see how the disorder of the "I" forces worked through the individual Sibyls and comes to expression in many different ways. Moreover, Michelangelo set up beside the sibylline powers, as a polar opposite, those who had attempted to seek the "I," to discover the "I" in human nature and to make it fertile for the historical development of humanity: these are the prophets. In Michelangelo, the Sibyls and the prophets represent both polarities: on the one side the tendency of the "I" to lapse into disorder, on the other, the seeking of the Hebrew prophets to bring the forces of the "I" into order. The real awakening to consciousness of the "I" that was to occur was fermenting in human nature, and if the danger had not been deflected, dark prophetic sibylline forces would be tumbling in confusion in our "I" today. A real clarity of the "I" would not have been possible in the development of the following centuries. Then the incarnation of Christ in Jesus of Nazareth occurred at the time of this fermentation and brought about for the fourth time the harmonizing of human nature. This could only happen because the Christ being incarnated in a human being, who had developed in the highest sense the capacities accessible to human beings at that time.

Just as modern esoteric research makes it possible to cast light on the four stages of the Mystery of Golgotha, it also puts us in a position to throw light on the nature of Jesus of Nazareth, in whom the Christ being incarnated through the Mystery of Golgotha, the fourth and last stage. I drew attention on earlier occasions to the fact that at the beginning of our time reckoning two Jesus infants were born. I pointed out that in the twelfth year of one of the boys, who was descended from the Nathan line of the house of David, the soul of the other Jesus boy, who was of the Solomon line, took up residence, so that the two Jesus boys became one being. If we ask ourselves who this twelve-year-old Jesus of Nazareth was, then modern esoteric research answers that it was the soul of Zoroaster in a very special human being, who was descended from the Nathan line of the house of David. And if we now turn our spiritual gaze to the being of Zoroaster in the Nathan Jesus, we see how this Jesus of Nazareth developed further up until his thirtieth year.

We can distinguish three periods in the development of this Jesus of Nazareth: the first from the twelfth to the eighteenth year, the second from the eighteenth to the twenty-fourth year, and the third from about the twenty-fourth year to the thirtieth year. The young Jesus of Nazareth lived in the house headed by his real father and the mother of the Solomon Jesus boy. Both his birth mother and the father of the Solomon Jesus boy had died in the meantime. The young Jesus of Nazareth was brought into the trade of his father, a sort of cabinet and carpentry workshop. Besides this, however, he developed remarkably in his soul, with infinite perfection in spiritual life. We must bear in mind that no one from his family understood the deeply significant development of the young Jesus of Nazareth. Already as a boy of twelve to eighteen years, he was isolated with it, entirely alone with it. This inner development, which was accomplished in the loneliness of the soul, was remarkable because Jesus of Nazareth could bring up, as from the deep foundation of his soul, all the great revelations that had come to the Hebrew people over the course of time. At the time when Jesus of Nazareth lived, the people of Israel had hardly anything but the written records of what the ancient prophets had once received in direct revelation from the spiritual worlds. They knew from the texts what the ancients had received as revelations, but they no longer had any possibility of reaching the revelations themselves, which had once come to the ancient prophets through the voice one called the great Bath-Kol.† Jesus of Nazareth experienced in himself, as in a reversed development, everything the Hebrew people had lived through, and he developed himself to the point that his soul sensed: "The great Bath-Kol is speaking to me again. I am perceiving, directly from the spiritual world, the voice the prophets once received."

And as happens with a spiritual development of this sort, this inner development was connected with the deepest pain and suffering. The human being does not gain the highest knowledge without pain and suffering. One experience specifically was stored up in the soul of the roughly seventeen to eighteen-year-old Jesus of Nazareth, as he recognized: "Once the great Bath-Kol pronounced the most wonderful revelations to the Hebrew people. But if the great Bath-Kol were to speak to the Hebrew people today, no one would hear it. They understand the scripture, but they no longer understand the living scripture." He was lonely within himself; a vast sadness came over his soul for what had become of his people in the declining evolution of humanity.

Then came the time when Jesus of Nazareth was to be sent out into the world. He wandered, practicing his craft here and there, in different areas, within Palestine as well as outside it in pagan areas. In his wanderings Jesus made a remarkable impression on the people he encountered. What had caused the pain in this soul had been transformed into something like love, which the people felt streaming out from him when in his presence. When, in his way, he sat in the evenings after finishing his work with the people he visited, they felt as if an atmosphere of love came over them—with his words, but also with his mere presence. What was imbued with love, what he could discuss with them, made the deepest impression on people, and when he had gone away to work somewhere else, something like the most lively remembrance of him remained behind with those he had left. It often happened that the people whom Jesus of Nazareth had left three of four weeks before had a common vision that he came to them once again and spoke with them—the vision spoke with them. So deep was the impression that this Jesus of Nazareth made that he had basically remained with them! What Jesus of Nazareth was imprinted itself on hundreds and thousands of souls as he wandered about in his eighteenth to twenty-fourth years.

In this wandering, Jesus of Nazareth also went into pagan areas. He came one day to a place where the people were in despair. This place had been abandoned by its priests. There was a sacrificial altar, but it was desolate. The priests had fled because a vicious disease had broken out among the people. Such sacrificial altars and cultic rites were derived from the mysteries. What had been revealed in the mysteries had been carried over into the ceremonial acts at these sacrificial altars. To understand such a thing we must take note of the meaning of the ceremonial sacrifice. Through the way the sacrificial rituals were performed and the prayers that imbued them, spiritual forces really flowed down onto the altars. However, when Jesus came to the sanctuary, he found that the good forces that had once flowed down onto the altars during sacrifices were no longer there. He found that the sanctuaries, which had been abandoned by the priests, were populated by demonic powers gathered around the altar.

Even the desperate, sick, degraded people of this pagan place had a deep impression, as they noticed Jesus of Nazareth approaching, whom they did not know, but who poured out an atmosphere of love. At first they believed that one of their old priests had come back to offer up their pagan sacrifices. Jesus of Nazareth obviously did not want to perform the pagan sacrifices, but he walked among the people. There he was seized by the power of the demons around the altar and keeled over as if dead. When the people saw this, they fled. While falling into unconsciousness, Jesus of Nazareth saw the demonic powers pursuing them. Then he lost normal consciousness and was carried off into spiritual worlds where he could now perceive what had once been revealed to the priests of the ancient mysteries in purity and truth. He could perceive the ancient pagan revelations just as he had perceived the Hebrew revelations in the voice of Bath-Kol. And he could hear the ancient pagan revelation, which can be repeated in the language of today in roughly the following way:

AUM
AMEN.
Evils reign
Bearing witnesses to "I"-ness
Separating itself
And to selfhood's guilt—
Incurred through others,
Experienced in the daily bread
Wherein the will of heaven
Does not reign
Because humanity
Has separated itself
From forgotten your names
Ye Fathers in the Heavens.

And Jesus of Nazareth knew in his altered state of consciousness that this revelation flowed through the very ancient sacred teachings of the mysteries. He awakened, and retained the memory of what were once the ancient, sacred doctrines of the pagan religions. He then turned what he had received in this revelation around for the further progress of humanity, and it became the Lord's Prayer.

What one learns in relation to the higher worlds is not learned merely through doctrines, but much more through facts that one experiences in the higher worlds. The entire meaning of such a revelation is learned in an infinitely deeper way than one can ever learn through doctrines or theories. A new great pain was stored up in the soul of Jesus of Nazareth. He had before him an especially clear case of the miserable state of the pagan revelations, and now he could contrast it with what they had once been. And just as he could say in the midst of the Hebrew people that, even if the voice of the great Bath-Kol were to sound forth, he would be isolated with it because they could no longer understand it, now he could say in respect to these people that if the voices of the ancient pagan mysteries were to sound again everywhere, there would be no one there who could understand it. Thus, Jesus of Nazareth was destined to experience the declining development of humanity in the deepest anguish.

The story I have just told took place in Jesus of Nazareth's twenty-fourth year approximately. Shortly after that, he went back home. It was approximately the time when his father died in Nazareth.

While he was back at home in Nazareth between his twenty-fourth and thirtieth years, he came into contact with the Essenes, who had settlements in the immediate area. He did not actually become an Essene, but due to his deep soul life, through the great twofold anguish that had been stored in his soul and transformed into love, the Essenes accepted him and spoke with him often about their deepest secrets, which they otherwise would have spoken about only to their own, to initiates. Only to him did they speak of their deepest secrets. And among the Essenes he became acquainted with people who at that time aspired, through a special inner development, to climb up again to the point from which humanity had devolved downwards. He took in eagerly what he could learn from the Essenes about the human development for such an ascent.

One day, as he was leaving the house of the Essenes and went through the doorway, he had an especially notable vision. On either side of the doorway he saw two forms, which he later knew to be Lucifer and Ahriman. They ran away from the door into the rest of the world. Through what he had gone through in his own inner development, he was now so advanced that he could, so to speak, read the meaning of this flight of Lucifer and Ahriman from the Essenes' door in the occult script. He saw that it was still possible at that time for individual people to rise up to the spiritual heights through a special development of their souls. However, this could happen only at the expense of the rest of the humanity; for only a few elect could go through the Essene development, and they could do so only because others remained at lower levels. He knew that the Essenes freed themselves from Lucifer and Ahriman through their mystical development, and that Lucifer and Ahriman had therefore to flee from the Essene houses. They ran straight to the other people and attacked the rest of humanity all the more. And from this occult experience the third great pain came upon him, when he realized that, while certain especially elect people could ascend to what had been revealed to people earlier, they could only climb up at the expense of the rest of humanity. That almost tore his heart out, for he was filled with love for all people. As a result of the third pain he understood that in whatever way contemporary individuals rose to higher spiritual knowledge, this knowledge had to be taken away from the rest of the people as a result. However high a soul might climb, whatever it might know in order to share the experience of the Essenes, the other people on this broad Earth were far too wretched for this.

As Jesus of Nazareth experienced such things, he learned that his stepmother, or foster mother, had more and more understanding for his inner life. This was particularly the case since the death of his father. And while in earlier years he was alone and lonely within the family, now he had many conversations with his mother, in which he could speak of what he experienced in his soul. And a great, decisive conversation between Jesus of Nazareth and his mother took place in the thirtieth year of his life. One day he spoke to her of every bit of knowledge he had laid up in his soul since his twelfth year: hearing the voice of the great Bath-Kol, the cosmic Lord's Prayer, and the experience among the Essenes.

And he spoke to her in such a way that this conversation had a deeply shattering effect, even when deciphered later by esoteric research in the akashic chronicle. What he said reached his mother not just as words, but as living forces, which carried the essence of the soul of Jesus of Nazareth as if on wings into the essence of the soul of the mother. So deeply connected was Jesus of Nazareth with what he had to clothe in words that his suffering and his knowledge flowed with the words over into the heart and soul of his mother. And it was as if his mother were imbued with a new life; as if rejuvenated, she came to life anew.

Jesus of Nazareth, however, came into a totally different state of soul, so to speak. He had let his own "I" flow out in his words with which he was so intimately connected. The "I" of Zoroaster had left the three bodies, the physical, etheric, and astral bodies of Jesus of Nazareth, and the forces of the cosmos went to work within the three bodies. Without "I"-consciousness as in a dream, Jesus of Nazareth, who had breathed out his Zoroaster "I" in the conversation with his mother, was impelled on the way to John the Baptist.

Thus was he prepared, after giving up this Zoroaster "I," to take up the Christ being as his new "I." With that the Mystery of Golgotha, the fourth stage of the Christ events, was now prepared. It transpired during the three years in which Christ lived in the body of Jesus of Nazareth, up until the Mystery of Golgotha. First at the Whitsun event did the apostles awaken out of another state of consciousness and grasp what had transpired with Christ Jesus.

If we survey what is known at this time about the Christ being as a result of present-day esoteric research, can we then say that our heart and soul would be less shaken by these revelations for our time than by the revelations about Jesus and Christ of an earlier time? The esoteric science of our day puts us in the position of knowing something more and deeper of Jesus Christ than bygone centuries have known. We may well say that the form of Christ grows to cosmic proportions when we strive to know it with the means that modern spiritual science puts at our disposal.

Let us look back at what was given to an earlier humanity about Jesus Christ, for example, in the four Gospels. From an esoteric standpoint it is very clear to us that the men who wrote the Gospels, wrote them according to the inspirations of the ancient mysteries and out of an atavistic clairvoyance. I have referred to this in my book *Christianity as Mystical Fact.* Paul was the first to have an impression of the cosmic significance of Christ. He could perceive how the power of the Christ being flowed into the aura of the Earth. What struck Paul as a particular point in the knowledge of Christ can, if we deepen the esotericism of our time, dawn on us as useful for the further fields of knowledge of Christ. For the moment the vision of Paul is extended from the Mystery of Golgotha to its three precursors, the moment it is extended from what for Paul is almost only the awareness of Jesus of Nazareth to the life of Christ Jesus, then the Pauline method will spread, to a certain degree, from one single center out over the whole great manifestation of the life of Christ Jesus. The moment we can now in this way, through devoted esoteric research, come to the point of making the Pauline method so to speak a universal one for the knowledge of Christ, then a real advance in the knowledge of Christ has been accomplished.

I did not wish to speak abstractly about the development of progress in the understanding of Christ; rather I wanted to demonstrate concretely what sort of Christ knowledge can be attained through esoteric science today. It will have become apparent to us from today's discussion that spiritual science, as we mean it, can be an instrument for ever deeper knowledge of the Christ. It is to be hoped that when humanity has come so far in rejecting old religious ideas about Christ because of materialistic influences, then modern spiritual science will give Christ back to humanity once again. For this spiritual science is not speaking out of theories about Christ, but rather in consciousness of the very words of Christ: "I am with you until the end of the Earth's days." For Christ is poured into the aura of the Earth, in which we ourselves are embedded. He lives within it! And, just as the apostles once lived with Christ Jesus on the physical plane, so can we communicate and associate with him as a spiritual being in the Earth's aura, if we appropriate this possibility. We must only accustom ourselves to really grasping the living presence of Christ in the Earth's aura and not to identify Christianity as a mere teaching, a mere doctrine. Since the Mystery of Golgotha, Christ is here all around us. We can find him in the same world we are in, not in a physical form, but as a spiritual being.

And we can see that he is active as a being, independent of what people are capable of thinking about him. Have we not experienced how in councils and other places of dispute, the opinions and the doctrines about Christ have gone back and forth, and how people were not capable of getting things right with their thoughts about Christ? How many opinions about Christ have we endured! If the further development of the Christ impulse were dependent on the opinions of people, the situation would really be bad for this further development of the Christ impulse. This Christ impulse is in the evolution of the Earth as a living reality, and works in it as a reality, without regard for what people think about him.

In order to make this sort of thing present for us, let us look at the date of October 28, 312. At that time Constantine, the son of Constantius Chlorus, stood before the gates of Rome, which was ruled by Maxentius. Constantine approached Rome with his relatively smaller army, whereas Maxentius had a significantly larger army at his disposal. Maxentius was safe within the walls of Rome. Constantine advanced in the open field. The battle fought at that time decided the map of Europe. A person who studies the story in its depths will have to admit that on that occasion the ideas of the generals were not decisive, nor were the rational reasons of people, but something entirely different! Maxentius consulted the sibylline books and received as answer: "If you attack Constantine outside the gates of Rome, you will destroy Rome's greatest enemy." A proper oracle! And in the night preceding the battle Maxentius had a dream, which drove him to leave the secure position within the walls of Rome and to march against Constantine. However, Constantine also had a dream that night, which advised him to have the symbol of Christ carried in front of his army and to conquer in this sign. No rational grounds, no strategic reasons, no expertise in the nature of war played a role when it came to the decisive moment; rather, subconscious forces stood opposed to each other in Maxentius and Constantine. One may think whatever one likes about the merit, or lack of it, in Constantine's thinking. In the victory he won at that time, the impulse of Christ lived as a true, real force, which worked through the subconscious of human beings since the Mystery of Golgotha, regardless of what people thought about Christ.

This is only one of the many events that could be brought to attest to how the Christ impulse at first entered into the subconscious forces of the soul. These subconscious soul forces might otherwise have passed over into the sibylline and have worked its way to the surface. And while the superficial conscious soul forces press more and more for the loss of the understanding of Christ through the materialistic stream, the Christ works on in the subconscious forces of human souls, as he worked in Constantine and Maxentius.

Today it is necessary for us to become conscious of what has been working in the subconscious forces of the soul. We should consciously recognize the being that since the Mystery of Golgotha has been working in the Earth's aura in the souls of humanity and from this aura has determined the destiny of the evolution of the world and of humanity. By holding this in our consciousness, we understand the progress that human understanding has made in reference to the Christ, and we understand our own task in relation to the advances in the knowledge of Christ.

10

THE FOUR SACRIFICES OF CHRIST: THE THREE PRECURSORS OF THE MYSTERY OF GOLGOTHA

BASEL, JUNE 1, 1914[†]

FOR our present-day culture it is necessary above all things that we come more and more to a new knowledge of Christ, by letting the results of spiritual science work on us. And much that bears the official seal of Christianity is hostile toward this new knowledge of Christ. It is necessary that we understand more and more that we need a school of selflessness for our culture. A renewal of morality, a deepening of human moral life, can only come through schooling in selflessness. In accordance with the conditions of the present cycle of time, we can work through this school of selflessness only if we gain a penetrating understanding for real selflessness.

If we look at the evolution of the world, we can find no deeper understanding for selflessness than what was given us through the appearance of Christ on Earth. And to know Christ means to undergo the school of selflessness. To know Christ means making oneself familiar with all the impulses of human development that trickle into our soul in such a way that they glow through, warm through, and call up to active soul existence everything in the soul that is inclined to selflessness. Under the influence of materialism the selflessness of humanity was lost in a way, as will be understood in future ages of humanity. However, through absorption in the Mystery of Golgotha, the penetration of the knowledge of the Mystery of Golgotha with our whole feeling and soul being, we can once again acquire a culture of selflessness. We can come to understand that what Christ did for the development of the Earth is contained in the fundamental impulse of selflessness, and that what he can become for the conscious development of the human soul is the school of selflessness! We become aware of this best if we consider the Mystery of Golgotha in its broader context.

This Mystery of Golgotha took place, as we know, once within the physical development of the Earth. The being we recognize as the Christ being was incarnated once in a physical body, in the body of Jesus of Nazareth. However, this Mystery of Golgotha had three preliminary stages. Three times previously, something occurred in the spiritual world. So, to a certain extent, we have three mysteries of Golgotha, which did not yet take place on the physical plane. The fourth was the first to take place on the physical plane, and that is the one about which the Gospels and the letters of Paul tell us. This greatest event to happen on Earth was prepared by three spiritual events, with one event lying in the ancient Lemurian age and two in the Atlantean age. The fourth event lies in the post-Atlantean period and is our Mystery of Golgotha.

Although the three preceding events did not transpire on Earth, but in the super-earthly world, the power of these events made its way down to the Earth. We want to try to understand how the forces of the three preparatory events influenced the development of humanity.

In reference to our moral life, to our understanding of the world, and to what transpires in our consciousness soul, we must first become selfless. That is a task of our present culture for the future. Human beings must become more and more selfless. Therein lies the future of right moral life actions, the future of all acts of love that can occur through earthly humanity. Our conscious life is on the way to selflessness or must be on the way to selflessness. In a certain connection, however, there is in us already something essentially selfless. And it would be the greatest misfortune of human beings on Earth if they became as selfish in regard to certain parts of their being as must be the case in many respects today in connection with their moral, intellectual, and feeling life. If selfishness, for example, could seize our senses to the same degree it seizes our morals, this would be the greatest misfortune of human beings on Earth. For our senses work on our body in such a way that selflessness expresses itself in this effect of the senses.

We have eyes in our body. We see through these eyes. However, we see only because the eyes are selfless, because we don't notice them at all. We carry them in us, we see things, so to speak, straight through the eyes, but the eyes themselves are extinguished as such in our perception. It is the same with the other senses. We perceive the world, because our sense system is selfless. Let us assume that our eyes were selfish. What would then happen with human beings? If, for example, we approached a blue color and the eye functioned in such a way that it would not let the color through, but would hold the color within itself and drain it of all of its essence, then the blue would suck on the eye. If the eye could become so selfish as we are in our moral life, in the intellectual and feeling life, we would feel it like a sucking force in the eye. If we came near a red color and our eye did not behave in a selfless way, but rather demanded to experience the red within itself, the red would have an effect like piercing on our eye. And if our eye were selfish, we would experience a pain of sucking or piercing with all impressions. We would be well aware that we had eyes, but we would only perceive sucking or piercing pains. In reality, human beings of today go through the world and know that color and light effects are there, however, they do not need to think about the eye. It snuffs itself out selflessly during perception. And it is the same with the other senses.

Selflessness rules in our senses. However, the senses might not have arrived at this selflessness; their selflessness would have been taken from them in the Lemurian age if Lucifer had been able to act as a free agent in that time. The spirit spoken of by the biblical phrase "Your eye will be opened" has caused human beings to be displaced to a sphere of earthly life, in which their eyes, if they had developed under the influence of Lucifer, would have become selfish. And with each impression—and it would have been the same for the other senses—people would not have perceived the red color but would have shouted, "Ah, something is sticking me here!" And they would not have seen the blue color, but would have said, "Something is sucking on me." In the Lemurian period, this danger was warded off from the development of humanity. In the super-earthly worlds the being, who later incarnated in the body of Jesus of Nazareth through the Mystery of Golgotha, ensouled himself (I cannot say incarnated) in an archangelic being. So, while the Earth was going through the Lemurian age, a being lived in the spiritual heights, who—one would wish to say through a kind of heralding of the baptism by John—was created through Christ penetrating an archangel who sacrificed its soul nature. Thereby Christ released a force that worked its way into human development on Earth and caused a calming and harmonizing of the senses. Because today we can use our senses in such a way that they are selfless, we will gaze—if we have understood the facts concerning this and are thankful to the world-order—into primeval times and recognize that what we are as sense beings makes it possible that, instead of feeling pain through our senses, we perceive the magnificence of nature around us; this comes from the first Christ sacrifice. Through ensouling himself in an archangel, he produced the effect that diverted the danger of selfishness of the senses from the development of humanity. That was the first preliminary stage of the Mystery of Golgotha.

When human beings gaze at the magnificence of nature, at the starry heavens, at everything the Sun shines on, at what is all around them in the animal, mineral, and vegetable kingdoms, they will gradually learn to develop a deep, significant religious feeling and to be thankful for the first sacrifice of Christ in preparation for the Mystery of Golgotha. This sacrifice allows the senses to function without pain and to be the instrument for perceiving the magnificence of the world. And we can foresee a time when the observation and enjoyment of nature will be imbued with Christ. We will go out and refresh ourselves with the magnificent beauty of springtime or summer, or with the other wonders of nature, and will realize that as we perceive all this splendor of nature, we must be aware that it is not us, but the Christ in our senses who makes this possible.

In the first times of the Atlantean development, the selfishness wanted to seize hold of the life organs of the human organization, through the influence of Lucifer and Ahriman. Let us try to look at what is essential in our life organization. What is that essential element? We need only to think what happens to us when this element in the life organs is impaired. And it is impaired, when physical illnesses of the life organs appear. Then we begin to experience the selfishness of our lungs, our heart, stomach, and other organs. The minute we first feel the pain, we know that we have a stomach, a heart. We have immediate consciousness of the fact that being sick means an organ has become selfish; it lives its own individual life in our organism. That is not the case in normal human life. Then the individual organ lives selflessly in the overall human organization. And our everyday constitution only keeps us on our feet in the world with certainty when we can go through the world with selfless organs, when we do not sense that we have a stomach, lungs, and so forth—when we have them without noticing them, when they don't start asserting themselves, when they are serving members in the whole organism.

On another occasion we will speak about why illness is brought about through the selfishness of the organs; today there will only be mention of the normal condition. If it were up to Lucifer and Ahriman, entirely other conditions would already have appeared in the Atlantean development. Each individual human organ would have become egotistical, and something quite peculiar would have happened. Let us assume that we approach some kind of fruit or something in the outside world that we can enjoy, or that stands in some kind of relationship to our bodily organization. Just this relationship to our life organs will be a subject of medical study when science finally allows itself to be stimulated by spiritual science. Then it will be known, for example, that when a person plucks cherries from the tree and eats them, what passes over into the organization has a special relationship to certain organs; other fruits and foods have other relationships to other organs. Everything that comes into the human organization has specific relationships to this organization.

If what was about to happen in the Atlantean period through Lucifer and Ahriman had been fulfilled, then when we picked the cherries, the organ that has a connection to the cherries would have felt intense craving of the highest degree. An infinite craving would have come to expression, and we would have sensed the relevant organ, which had selfishly stepped out of its place in the overall organism. However, because of this disruption, the other organs within the organism would have struggled just as selfishly. Or let us take another case, for example, if something were present which is harmful to us. Exactly as some things in the environment have specific connections with a person in a good sense, other things in the environment have detrimental ones. If we approached any sort of poisonous plant or something else that has only a detrimental relationship to one of our organs, we would have sensed this relationship through the inner activity of the organ. This would be expressed in a dreadful, tormenting feeling of fear. We would feel: here is something that so works on the organ that it makes it feel virtually burned out.

Let us now take not what people eat, but the air that surrounds us. Everything that appears in the air has a relationship to our organs. Had what Ahriman and Lucifer wanted come to fruition and had human beings been left to rely entirely on themselves, they would have been driven through the world between bestial greed for what is beneficial for one or the other organ and terrible disgust toward what is harmful for one organ or the other. Let us imagine that we were so situated in the world, with such physical organs, that we would be, to the highest degree, at the mercy of every pleasant aroma, running after it even if we were a hour away, or that a feeling of repulsion from far away would make it necessary for us to run away. If we were thrown back and forth like a rubber ball, how could we develop in the world? That things did not turn out that way, that our life organs were muted and harmonized, is the result of the second preliminary stage of Golgotha, which took place in super-earthly spheres when human beings were going through the first Atlantean period.

Again the Christ being ensouled itself in an archangelic being, and what was brought about through it radiated down into the Earth's atmosphere. That was when the harmonizing and the dampening down of the life organs that makes the human organs selfless took place. If this second Christ event had not intervened, our relationship with the environment would have continually caused the worst diseases; we could not be healthy at all. Future humanity will become selfless, if it can imbue itself with a real understanding of the spiritual world and acquire a feeling of gratitude for the spiritual beings on which the human being depends. Humanity will fill itself with the true piety through which it will understand that physical human beings with selfless organs do not exist only because they alone have developed themselves in the world, but because the Christ in them formed them in such a way that they can be human. We are learning more and more that we must fundamentally understand everything that makes us human in a global sense, so that we say, "Not I, but the Christ in me." Christ has taken care of the entire development of humanity in the three preliminary stages of the Mystery of Golgotha, which he accomplished before the actual Mystery of Golgotha.

In the last period of Atlantean development, humanity stood before a third danger. Thinking, feeling, and willing were about to lapse into disorder. Selfishness was about to move into thinking, feeling, and willing. What would have come about through that? Now, human beings might have wanted this or that, might have followed this or that impulse of the will, while their thinking would have followed another impulse, and their feeling yet another. It was necessary for the development of humanity that thinking, feeling, and willing fit themselves selflessly into the totality of the soul. This would have been impossible under the influence of Lucifer and Ahriman alone. In that case, thinking, feeling, and willing would have been selfish; they would have in a way torn apart the harmonious functioning of the soul. However, toward the end of the Atlantean development the third Christ event intervened. Once again the Christ being ensouled itself in an archangelic being, and the force that arose in the super-earthly world as a result harmonized thinking, feeling, and willing. Truly, just as the physical rays of the Sun must do their job on Earth so that all plant life does not wither away, so the Sun-Spirit must do its work, reflecting into the Earth from the super-earthly worlds, as I have just described. In the third stage the Christ being harmonized thinking, feeling, and willing, as they must be harmonized for normal human life.

What would have become of human beings if this third Christ event had not occurred? They would have been seized, as if by the Furies, by wild appetites and by the life of their will. They could have been seized by raving, in spite of the fact that their intellect, on the other hand, would have scorned what the will accomplished in its frenzy. This chaos was averted when the Christ being was in the soul of an archangel for the third time.

Humanity has received a memento of how human passion and human thinking were harmonized through the forces that acted from the super-earthly worlds. And this memento still exists, but is not understood in the right way. St. George defeating the dragon, or Michael defeating the dragon, is the sign formed for the third Christ event. St. George and Michael are the signs for Christ's ensouling of himself in the form of an archangel, and the dragon they destroy is the being who would have brought human thinking, feeling, and willing into disorder. All those who contemplate St. George with the dragon or Michael with the dragon, or something similar, are, in fact, contemplating the third Christ event. And the Greeks, who created in their wonderful mythology something like facsimiles of what transpired at the end of the Atlantean age in the spiritual world, revered the Sun-Spirit as the harmonizer of thinking, feeling, and willing in the human being. They understood that the Sun-Spirit had been ensouled in an etheric spirit form, the form of the beings we call archangels today. They understood that he created harmony on his wonderful lyre, making the human soul sound forth in harmony what otherwise would have been chaotic, wild, and ungoverned in the human soul as thinking, feeling, and willing. In Greece the Sun-Spirit became the guardian spirit of the human passions, which would have stormed fiercely, if they had come to life in the wild steam clouds rising out of the bowels of the Earth. If human beings had allowed only these steam clouds to act upon them, then thinking, feeling, and willing would have raged in a confused manner within them. So the Greek placed the Pythia over the steam clouds that rose out of the Earth and, through Lucifer and Ahriman, would bring the passions into disorder. But Apollo spread his light over Pythia and defeated the wildness of the passions. And she became a prophetess. The Greek felt the Sun-spirit Apollo to be the Christ of the third Christ event. In Apollo's protection in relationship to the passion-ruling temperament of the Pythia, the Greeks saw the effect of the third sacrifice of Christ in which the human passions that were lapsing into disorder were harmonized. For the Greeks, the Sun-spirit Apollo is basically the same as what is represented in the pictures of Michael or St. George, who conquer the dragon.

So we see that when Justin the Martyr makes a peculiar utterance, it makes sense—an utterance which, though the Martyr made it, may be regarded as Christian, although various contemporary representatives of Christianity would denounce him as a heretic. Justin said: "Heraclitus,

Socrates, and Plato were also Christian,[†] however only such as one could be before the Mystery of Golgotha." The theologians of today know nothing about this any more, but the Christian martyrs of the first period of Christianity still knew that the ancient Greek wise men, even if they did not perhaps use the name of Christ, would have known from their knowledge of the mysteries that Apollo was the great Sun-spirit, who would later live in a human being. If asked who Apollo was, they would have said that the Sun-Spirit was ensouled in Apollo, as in an archangelic form.

And then came the fourth, the earthly mystery, that of Golgotha. The same Christ being that had ensouled itself three times in the form of an archangel incarnated in the body of Jesus of Nazareth through the baptism by John in the Jordan. I concede that it will appear unusual to you when I say that this being has ensouled itself three times in the form of an archangel and then incarnated in a human form. For it would be more systematic to say that between the ensoulment in the form of an archangel and the incarnation in a physical body was an ensoulment in the form of an angel, meaning the Christ would have ensouled himself in an angelic form at one of the stages. That is how it would seem. However, when one hears people impute that the things coming from spiritual science are made up, truly it is not so. You can deduce this from other things. And if you ask me today how is it that the Christ did not descend from hierarchy to hierarchy, and then finally to the human, I must answer that I don't know, because I am definitely not drawing any conclusions. The fact is that Christ made use of an archangel form three times and then a human form; the angel form was omitted. I leave it to later research to determine why it is so. Today I do not yet know why, but it is true. If one wanted to invent, one would make it totally different[†]; that you can infer from what has just been said.

And so the fourth stage of the Mystery of Golgotha took place. This Mystery of Golgotha averted the danger that the "I" would lapse into disorder through the influence of Lucifer and Ahriman. In ancient Lemuria, the sense organs would have lapsed into disorder through Lucifer; in the first Atlantean period disorder and disharmony threatened the life organs; in the last Atlantean period the organs of the soul (*Gemüt*) which underpin thinking, feeling, and willing. And in the post-Atlantean age disorder threatened the "I" itself. Because the "I" was to make strides in human development at this time, one sought to produce harmony between this "I" and the forces of the cosmos, so that the "I" would not be the mere plaything of these forces. This could have happened. The "I" would have taken such a form that it would have been impossible to keep hold of one's self, and if given over to these forces, whatever would come from the soul would have been swept along in all directions with all the elemental forces that come from wind, air, and waves.

Michelangelo painted it. Take a look at the Michelangelo's pictures, and you will see that he painted the Sibyls as that which threatened the human being. He depicted so wonderfully, how they represent the type of person who feels the "I" lapsing into disorder, so that when this "I" comes into disorder, all the wonderful wisdom possible can come forth, but in such a way that the human being cannot direct it. They represent the different stages of what is given over to elemental beings through disorder of the "I." On the other hand, however, something else emerges. In the same space he painted the meditating forms of the prophets, on whom we can see that they bring to light that which maintains the order of the "I" over against the cosmos. It can move us deeply when we see the drive toward the "I" in the prophets, and on the other side the human beings who have come into disorder through the "I" itself, and then see Christ himself in this space, who incarnated in a human body and whose task is to bring the "I," which is about to come into the world, into order.

Yes, spiritual science will show us ever more profoundly how this human "I" can arrive at selflessness through the fourth Christ event, the Mystery of Golgotha. The senses have said, "Not I, the Christ in us." The life organs have said, "Not I, the Christ in us." The organs of the mind have said, "Not I, the Christ in us." The moral and intellectual life of human beings must learn to say, "Not I, the Christ in me." Every step into the spiritual world shows us this.

I wanted to deal with this today, so that we can on another occasion, which we will hopefully have very soon, give individual esoteric proofs for these facts, and show how what we call spiritual science will pour into our moral and intellectual life in such a way that human beings will become pupils of selflessness, that the Christ will live in us, and that we will feel the living Christ in every word spoken about spiritual science.

There is only one more thing to add. You know that we have performed our Mystery Dramas in Munich since 1909.† One may find what is presented on the mystery stage good or bad, but that is not the issue now. What has been done needed a certain power, a power that does not just come to a person, because he or she is a human being on the Earth. You see, if we want to be able to work here in Dornach, if we want to be able to work with and process our various kinds of hardwood, we need physical strength.† We cannot say that we can deliberately give ourselves this physical strength. It comes from our body and from what we can do in our soul. It is out of our hands. Moreover, all that we carry out in the spiritual sphere, for which we need spiritual power, is out of our hands. That doesn't depend on our human talents alone, just as whether we can do something on Earth does not depend on our talents alone, but also on the physical strength of our body. So we need spiritual powers, which are just as much outside us as the physical strength is outside of our soul. I know that shallow people can come along and say, "You are a fool, because you believe that spiritual forces come to you from outside, whereas they only rise up from within oneself." Let them consider me a fool. I find they have the kind of cleverness that cannot tell hunger from a piece of bread.

I know how spiritual powers flow into a person from without. Just as we could only believe that hunger itself creates the bread that satisfies it if we were crazy, so little does the power of our soul create the powers we need for spiritual activity. They must flow into us; they must flow to us. And just as we know perfectly well, if we are not crazy, that hunger is in us and that the bread comes from without, just so do those who live in the spiritual world know what is inside them and what comes from outside. As for myself, increasingly since 1909, when it came to developing quietly and slowly what was necessary for the Mystery Dramas, I felt the spiritual power that came from outside. I knew the spiritual eye of a spiritual being was resting on what was done. And I say this out of direct experience.

In the early days of our work in spiritual science, a person came to us as a friend† and took up with a wonderful enthusiasm what we had to offer back then. But it was not only with a wonderful, devoted enthusiasm that she took up what we were able to offer about the development of humanity, cosmic secrets, and about reincarnation and karma; rather she united it at the same time with a wonderful esthetic sense. Everything experienced in teaching or in conversing with this personality was immersed in beauty. There were still only a few of us back then. We had no need yet to squeeze ourselves into the space, as is the case today. And the things we speak about before a great audience today were back then discussed by only three: myself and two others.† One of these people died already in 1904. It is so, that such persons go through a development after death. In the year 1907, as we performed Schuré's reconstruction of the mystery of Eleusis at our congress,† there was not yet any perceptible sign of an influence from this soul. It began in 1909 and has been coming more and more since then. I know precisely that it is the individuality of our friend, purely because of the kind of individual traits one could cherish truly and objectively. In the spiritual world, she acted as a guardian angel for what we had to achieve in the uniting of the esthetic and the esoteric in our Mystery Dramas. We felt what passed over from her into our earthly activity and what flowed into effectiveness on the Earth and penetrated us, to be well protected by this personality who died in 1904. We look up with gratitude, for what was accomplished came about because the soul eye of a spiritual personality rested upon our deeds.

However, then, when it became a matter of cultivating what one can call dialogue (because it is a kind of activity of exchange), it was always, over and over again, a situation in which this personality revealed that she could find her way to our activity on Earth all the better, the more we imbued ourselves with the thought of Christ in the evolution of the Earth. If I were to put into earthly words what this individuality was constantly saying, I would say (I must express this only symbolically, for it is very different in the spiritual world), "I find my way to you so well, because you are finding the way more and more to make your spiritual science an expression of the living Word of Christ."

The Christ impulse will become for us the living bridge between the life of the Earth and the life in super-earthly worlds. Three times Christ laid into human beings from out of the spiritual world that nature which they needed to live properly, making their sense, life, and soul (*Gemüt*) organs selfless. Now it is up to human beings themselves to become selfless in the intellectual and moral aspects by learning to understand for this intellectual and moral life the saying "Not I, but Christ in me."

The world will recognize that what we proclaim as spiritual science is the Word of Christ. He has said, "I am with you always until the end of the Earth." The mission of spiritual science in our time is to open the gates to the living Christ. United with the understanding of the living are the dead, who know that Christ has found the passage from heaven to earthly activity. And when the dead incline themselves as the closest protecting gods toward those who live on Earth, they find them all the more intensively, the more these souls are themselves imbued and inspired by the Christ impulse. The Christ descended as the lofty Sun-Spirit from the super-earthly world through the Mystery of Golgotha, to find a dwelling in human souls. Spiritual science should become the glad tidings of how the Christ can find a dwelling in the souls of human beings. When the Christ finds a dwelling in the souls of earthly human beings, then the Christ force will shine back once again from the Earth's aura into the worlds Christ left for the salvation of people on Earth, and the entire cosmos will be permeated with Christ.

We bring ourselves gradually such a deep understanding of the Mystery of Golgotha by penetrating it with spiritual science. If we reflect on it in that way, and think, in addition, about how it must be a school of selflessness for the intellectual and moral life of humanity on into the future, then will we be intensely permeated with the need for the spiritual-scientific proclamation of the Mystery of Golgotha! Then will we know what is meant by the spiritual-scientific impulses that desire to enter into the present. Then will the Christ impulse penetrate humanity. In truth, all people can accept him, because Christ did not appear in one nation, but is rather the lofty Sun being who belongs to the entire Earth and can penetrate all human souls, regardless of their nationality or religion. May there eventually be a good many people who find the way to such an understanding of the Christ impulse and to such an understanding of the Mystery of Golgotha. Then perhaps will that be considered to be Christian, which today is called unchristian and heretical by many who fancy themselves to be Christian.

If we attempt to attain not merely an intellectual understanding of the Mystery of Golgotha, but rather to take hold of this Mystery of Golgotha with our entire soul, then we need spiritual science to do it. Then, however, we will realize ourselves as members of our spiritual stream, as those souls who understand what is necessary for humanity now and in the immediate future.

These are the things about which I wished to speak to you today. Hopefully, there will be an opportunity to come back to this city sometime relatively soon, to lecture further on the theme we have been discussing here.

EDITORIAL AND REFERENCE NOTES

The title of this volume and the titles of the individual lectures do not come from Rudolf Steiner. In his lifetime only the two London lectures of May 1 and 2, 1913, appeared in print.

Textual sources: The lectures were for the most part written down by members incompletely trained in stenography. Although the writers submitted a polished text, these notes should not be taken as entirely free of lacunae or errors. Only the copyists of the following lectures are known by name: Stuttgart, May 18 and 20, 1913: Agnes Friedländer and Clara Michels. Stuttgart, March 5, 1914: Grete Kreuzhage. Basel, June 1, 1914: Rudolf Hahn.

Textual differences from the first edition: For the two lectures in Stuttgart, May 18 and 20, 1913, only the edited work of Agnes Friedländer was available for the first German edition. For the present edition the copy of Clara Michels was added. The changes were derived from a comparison of these copies. In the lecture in London, May 2, 1913, it was possible to insert, on the basis of a copy by Pieter de Haan, Holland, the section on p. 29 "The seeds of ... in the twentieth century."

On the subjects of the lectures: After Rudolf Steiner in the lectures in London, May 2, 1913, and Stuttgart, May 20, 1913, had spoken of a second Mystery of Golgotha that took place in the course of the nineteenth century, the communication about the preliminary stages of this Mystery of Golgotha in earlier epochs of humanity appeared first in the cycle *Christ and the Spiritual World. Of the Quest for the Holy Grail* (held at New Year's 1913/14 in Leipzig), CW 140.* The subsequent presentations given in other places—the last at Basel on Easter Monday, June 1, 1914—are contained in the present volume.

With the results of these researches it is a question nonetheless of only one motif from the new understanding of Christ by Rudolf Steiner, for which reason a few others that stand in close relation to it could be mentioned:

The Event of the Christ-Appearance in the Etheric World (16 lectures in various cities, 1910), CW 118;

Esoteric Christianity and the Spiritual Guidance of Humanity (23 lectures in various cities, 1911–12), CW 130.

The Fifth Gospel: From the Akashic Record (18 lectures in various cities, 1913–14), CW 148.

---

* Works of Rudolf Steiner mentioned here and in the following notes are indicated by their bibliographical number (CW) in the Collected Works series. Please refer to the summary of Rudolf Steiner's Collected Works, starting on p. 143.

1.
Esoteric Science and Esoteric Development—Initiation

Page 1, "visiting this country..."
After the founding of the Anthroposophical Society. Rudolf Steiner had last visited London in July 1905 on the occasion of the Second Congress of the Federation of European Sections of the Theosophical Society.

Page 2, "akasha."
For Rudolf Steiner, the akasha or akashic chronicle is a living chronicle of what takes place on Earth recorded in a subtle, delicate essence. Lasting impressions of what is thought, felt and willed, what passes into deeds, are inscribed so that what is spiritually active within us and has flowed into the physical is there to be seen in the spiritual. This chronicle can be "read" by the initiate. See particularly CW 99.

Page 5, "in the ancient Lemurian epoch..."
Lemuria is the third period of development of the Earth stage of our Earth. The Earth progresses in its evolution through seven planetary stages: old Saturn, old Sun old Moon, Earth, Jupiter, Venus and Vulcan. The current planetary stage is the Earth Stage, which has seven epochs: Polarean, Hypoborean, Lemurian, Atlantean, post-Atlantean and a sixth and seventh after that. Our current epoch is the post-Atlantean which, in turn, has seven cultural ages: ancient Indian, ancient Persian, Babylonian-Chaldean, Greek-Roman, fifth post-Atlantean (ours), the sixth post-Atlantean (Philadelphia) and the seventh post-Atlantean age. In the middle of Lemuria is the point where the soul begins to ensoul the body from within. See CW 11 and CW 13 for detailed descriptions of this sequence of evolution.

Page 7, "Ernst Haeckel and Herbert Spencer..."
Ernst Haeckel (1834–1919), a German zoologist.
Rudolf Steiner had felt no need to meet Haeckel, but when Steiner attended the festivities for Haeckel's 60th birthday he was introduced to him at his request. In a conversation Haeckel said to him: "People say that I deny the spirit. I wish they could see how various materials shape themselves through their own forces; then they would perceive 'spirit' in everything that happens in a laboratory retort. Spirit is everywhere." (From CW 28.) Steiner said of this that Haeckel had absolutely no idea what spirit is. He thought the forces of nature were spirit.

In 1900 and 1901, Steiner dedicated his *Conceptions of the World and of Life in the Nineteenth Century*, later expanded and titled *The Riddles of Philosophy*, to Ernst Haeckel, in spite of the fact that his thinking, and so the content of the book, was so very different from that of Haeckel.

Just when Haeckel had formulated his monism in his talk, "Monism as the Bond between Religion and Science," he heard that Rudolf Steiner was in Weimar and sent a copy of his talk to him. Steiner returned the favor by sending Haeckel a copy of the magazine containing the talk he had given in Vienna against Haeckel's monism.

Rudolf Steiner said of Ernst Haeckel's work: "Haeckel's research results build, so to speak, the first chapter of theosophy or spiritual science. One can find one's way into the origin and transformation of the organic forms better when one studies his works than through anything else." (From CW 54).

It is a first chapter because, "Haeckel can only see what the senses grasp and how it changes. What is and changes in this way he can acknowledge as his reality, and he is only satisfied when he is able to comprise the entire human being, including his thought activity, under this concept of being and transformation." (From the "Introduction to the 1923 Edition" of CW 18) Here spiritual science begins its task of gaining knowledge beyond the threshold or limits of the physical senses.

Haeckel saw the animal as the ancestor of the human being, whereas Rudolf Steiner's spiritual research shows that the animal and the human being have the same primordial ancestor, with the evolutionary divergence coming about through the fact that those that could develop farther became human beings, and those that could not, separated out and became animals.

Herbert Spencer (1820–1903) a British philosopher, attempted to build a philosophical theory based on the natural scientific findings of his day, which would then apply to all areas of life and the world.

In CW 18 Rudolf Steiner pointed out that Herbert Spencer believed there was an unknowable absolute, but went on to say, "The field, however, that Spencer considers to be accessible to knowledge must, for him, entirely take on the form of natural scientific conceptions. When Spencer himself ventures to explain, he does so in the sense of natural science.

"Spencer uses the method of natural science in thinking of the process of knowledge. Every organ of a living being has come into existence through the fact that this being has adapted itself to the conditions under which it lives. It belongs to the human conditions of life that man finds his way through the world with the aid of thinking. His organ of knowledge develops through the adaptation of his conceptual life to the conditions of his external life. By making statements concerning things and processes, man adjusts himself to the surrounding world. All truths have come into being through this process of adaptation, and what is acquired in this way can be transmitted through inheritance to descendants. Those who think that man, through his nature, possesses once and for all a certain disposition toward general truths are wrong. What appears to be such a disposition did not exist at an earlier stage in the ancestors of man, but has been acquired by adaptation and transmitted to the descendants...." (From CW 18)

For more about their theories, see CW 4, CW 18, and CW 54.

Page 8, "Broca's area..."
In 1861 Paul Broca discovered that when the brains of people who had a speech impediment are dissected after death, something in the left third convolution of the brain is damaged. This area is associated with speech, as the speech organ in the brain.

Page 11, "How to Know Higher Worlds..."
Formerly titled *Knowledge of Higher Worlds and Its Attainment.*

2.
Christ at the Time of the Mystery of Golgotha and Christ in the Twentieth Century

Page 24, "Christ...in the body of Jesus...among people of the Earth."
For a detailed account of the preparation for and incarnation of Christ in Jesus at the baptism in the Jordan, see CW 114 and CW 123.

Page 26, "Within the last couple of decades, Michael..."
The Age of Michael began in 1879 A.D.

Page 29, "in the sense of the Manichaean principle."
Manichaean Principle: the transformation of evil into the good through love. In the view of the Manichaeans, good and evil are not seen as two absolute opposites that cannot be united, with the one shutting the other out. Evil is an integral part of the cosmos. It works on the evolution of the cosmos and must, in the end, be absorbed, transformed, by the good.

3.
The Michael Impulse and the Mystery of Golgotha (1)

Page 32, "in two lectures..."
In CW 140.

Page 33, "as we heard yesterday..."
Public lecture, Stuttgart, May 17, 1913: "Results of Spiritual Research for Questions of Life and the Riddle of Death."

Page 35, "in the ancient Saturn period,"
See note to page 5.

Page 36, "in Kristiana on the development of the different people..."
In CW 121.

Page 43, "Buddha."
See note to page 33.

4.
The Michael Impulse and the Mystery of Golgotha (2)

Page 45, "yesterday in the public lecture."
Lecture in Stuttgart, May 19, 1913, in CW 69.

Page 52, "the evolution that the Buddha has undergone."
In CW 130 and CW 140.

Page 52, "reservations...against us..."
Allusion to the efforts of the Theosophical Society splinter group "Star of the East" to promote the young Indian Krishnamurti as the Christ bearer.

5.
Christ's Path through the Centuries

Page 57, "holy Rishis..."
The Holy Rishis were seven pupils of Manu. He wove into their life bodies (etheric bodies) the etheric bodies of the seven leaders of the Atlantean epoch that had been permeated by archangels and that had been preserved on ancient Atlantis. These seven Holy Rishis were sent by Manu to found the first post-Atlantean culture: the ancient Indian culture. They bestowed upon humanity the recollection of the Atlantean cultures but in a new form. See lecture on April 16, 1909 in CW 110 and lecture on April 13, 1912 in CW 136. Also lecture on December 13, 1908 in CW 108.

Page 58, "The fifth age..."
Refers to the fifth post-Atlantean Age.

Page 60, "Immanuel Kant."
1724–1804. On Rudolf Steiner's treatment of Kant's philosophy compare especially CW 4 and CW 19.

Page 60, "about a 'fifth gospel.'"
See CW 148.

Page 61, "about the two boys named Jesus…"
Rudolf Steiner spoke about it for the first time in the lectures in Basel of September 15 to 26, 1909, in CW 114. There is also a presentation in CW 15.

Page 61, "religious traditions are no longer taught in school…"
Rudolf Steiner was speaking here of the schools in Europe. Today in the United States, because of the separation of church and state, religious instruction is not permitted in the public schools.

Page 62, "as far as the Germanic peoples…"
On this see the detailed presentations in the lecture on January 11, 1919, in CW 188.

Page 63, "Tauler, Meister Eckhart and Jakob Böhme."
Both Meister Eckhart (1260–1328) and Johannes Tauler (1300–1361) were Dominican monks. Meister Eckhart became professor of theology at the Dominican College in Cologne, Germany, shortly after Tauler began his studies there.

In his travels, Tauler came into contact with members of the Friends of God, a famous group of mystics. This and other meetings with the Friends of God had an important effect on his life and work.

Jakob Böhme was a master shoemaker from Görlitz, Germany. The resurrection of the divine soul in the ordinary human soul was a direct experience for Jakob Böhme.

For more about these mystics see CW 7, also on Jakob Böhme on May 3, 1906 in CW 54.

Page 63, "a renowned theologian…"
Arthur Drews (Ütersen/Holstein 1865–1935, Achern). See "Berlin Discussion of Religion. Did Jesus Live? Lectures on the Myth of Christ," held on January 31 and February 1, 1910 by Arthur Drews and others, Berlin and Leipzig, 1910. He was a German philosopher who was professor at the Polytechnic Academy in Karlsruhe. He supported concrete monism. Rudolf Steiner also spoke of him in the lecture of October 30, 1921, in CW 208, Vol. 2, as being unable to move from word to concept, and so being among those who set aside the truth in their attempts to develop a theory.

6.
The Three Spiritual Preliminary Stages of the Mystery of Golgotha

Page 68, "on the fifth Gospel…"
See the Stuttgart lecture of November 22, 1913 in CW 148.

Page 69, "consumed within with agony."
After this sentence there is a lacuna in the transcription. Also, see the general comments about the other lectures in this volume ("Textual sources," page 133).

Page 73, "Gnosis."
The Gnostics could not conceive of the Christ Being incarnating into and indwelling Jesus. They had no understanding of the connection of their own higher being with their own physical being.

"Gnosis was a remnant of ancient wisdom arising out of an atavistic knowledge of the spiritual worlds in the days of early humankind. Those who possessed this ancient wisdom, which was still understood by the Gnostics at the time of the Mystery of Golgotha, knew that it contained a view—the names were different then—of the hierarchies which underlie the creation of the world, and they were able to conceive of the significance of Christ. Together with the Gnosis, there disappeared the possibility of comprehending the Christ being as a cosmic being. Instead, there remains dogma which has perpetuated certain incomprehensible concepts—the Credo, and so on—about the Christ being.

"What was important in centuries gone by was not so much the wisdom about Christ as the fact itself, the fact that Christ turned towards the Earth and fulfilled the Mystery of Golgotha. A true understanding of the Christ Being will first have to be won through the new Gnosis, which is something entirely different from the old Gnosis, for it is anthroposophical spiritual science." (From CW 173, Vol. 1)

Page 73, "devachan."
Devachan is the theosophical term for the spiritual world or the heavens.

Page 73, "Scotus Erigena..."
John Scotus Eruigena. Probably in Ireland ca. 810–ca. 877 in France. Translator of the writings of Dionysius the Areopagite, author of *De Divina Praedestinatione, De Divisione Naturae.* In 1225 the Vatican directed that his writings be burned.

Page 73, "Maid of Orleans."
See also CW 126 and CW 157.

Page 75, "moral imagination."
Chapter XII in CW 4.

7.
The Christ Impulse across the Ages and Its Power in the Human Being

Page 80, "the spirits of form..."
Spirits of form are also called exusiai or powers or elohim in other traditions.

Page 81, "my presentation...for the Lemurian period..."
See CW 11.

Page 86, "The fourth danger..."
In this section one should take into account that the transcribed text is obviously incomplete.

Page 88, "into upright walking, into speaking and into thinking..."
On this, see CW 15.

8.
The Christ Spirit and Its Relation to the Evolution of Consciousness

Page 92, "Lecture 8: Munich, March 30, 1914"
The words introducing this lecture about the construction at Dornach have been omitted here. They appear in CW 253.

Page 93, "The relation to Krishna..."
Presented in the lectures at Helsingfors, May 28–31, June 1–5, 1913, CW 146.

Page 94, "human senses (for there are twelve)..."
On this see the lectures in Berlin, October 23–27 1909, November 1–4, 1910, and December 12–16, 1911, in CW 115.

Page 97, "Thales, Pherecydes of Syros and Anaxagoras..."
Thales (c.650–c.560 B.C.) was a pre-Socratic Greek philosopher of Miletus, reputed founder of the Milesian or Ionian school of philosophy. He explained the physical world as deriving from a single underlying substance, which he believed to be water. Among his pupils were Anaxagoras and Diogenes. Thales was also a merchant, mathematician and astronomer.

In **Pherecydes of Syros** (6th century B.C.) we can observe the transition from the old picture-consciousness to the consciousness of thought. In his world picture-consciousness and thought-consciousness had an equal share. His view was that the world is constituted through the cooperation of three principles: Chronos, Chton, and Zeus. In modern terms Chronos could be thought of as time-creator, Chton as matter-producer, and Zeus as space-ether.

Anaxagoras (c.500–428 B.C.) was a Greek philosopher, thought to be the teacher of Socrates. He held that an all-pervading *nous* (world-reason) ordered the physical world by combining particles from the undifferentiated mass of the universe. See CW 18.

Page 97, "Christianity…always…one calls it Christianity now."
St. Augustine (354–430 AD), *Retractationes*, L. i, cap. 13.3.

Page 99, "Arthur Drews…"
See page 65.

Page 102, "of Eucken's philosophy."
Rudolf Eucken (1846–1926), a German philosopher. He directed his philosophical investigation to self-observation of the soul, observing those experiences of the soul that form the basis for the self-conscious ego, but did not penetrate to the sources in which the experiences of the soul originate. For a more detailed description of his philosophy, see CW 18. Also compare CW 19.

9.
Progress in the Knowledge of Christ: The Fifth Gospel

Page 104, "In today's discussion…"
Rudolf Steiner spoke in Paris on May 25, 26, and 27, 1914. The two lectures of May 25 and 26 on clairvoyance, reason, and science are in CW 154. On the lecture of May 27, 1914, see also CW 148.

Page 109, "Bath-Kol."
Hebrew, "daughter of the voices"; in Greco-Jewish scripture, "voices of heaven." According to the Talmud a kind of divine revelation, which took a second rank after prophecy.

10.
The Four Sacrifices of Christ: The Three Precursors of the Mystery of Golgotha

Page 118, "Lecture 10: Basel, June 1, 1914"
The introductory words to this lecture on the affairs of the Anthroposophical Society are omitted here. They appear in *What is Happening in the Anthroposophical Society*, 1936, no. 39 and in CW 252.

Page 126, "Justin the Martyr…utterance… 'Heraclitus, Socrates, and Plato were also Christian'…"
Justin the Martyr, *Apology for Christianity*, I.46. One of the Church Fathers. For more about Justin the Martyr, see lecture of October 8, 1911, in CW 131.

Page 126, "one would make it totally different..."
In this place in the first edition of the lecture Marie Steiner made the following note: "See the relevant passage in the published lecture cycle, *Christ and the Spiritual World: The Search for the Holy Grail* (CW 149). There Rudolf Steiner also speaks (one can't say everything in one lecture) about the angel-*like* being that lay at the foundation of the Nathan Jesus boy, which belonged to the soul material that stayed behind in the spiritual world when the real development of humanity began with its Luciferic intrusion. A relation remained between this purely spiritual substance and what was distributed among the individual human souls; it expressed itself in a spiritual protection of the human being from the attacks of Lucifer and Ahriman as it developed on the physical plane. That superhuman being decided to work through a development in the world of the upper hierarchies, which enabled it to be infused for a while with the Christ being. The spiritual Sun activity became subdued in a certain way through this in the activity of the cosmic forces for the purpose of harmonizing the human being on Earth. When Christ, at the ensoulment of the archangel form, connected himself with Jesus of Nazareth, he made him capable of ejecting the dragon from the nature of the human soul. The Greek gods are projections of that angel-like being in his progress through the planets.

Page 128, "Mystery Dramas in Munich since 1909."
From 1909 to 1913 mystery plays were performed in Munich every year: in 1909 *The Children of Lucifer* by Edouard Schuré; 1910–1013 the four "Mystery Dramas" (CW 14) by Rudolf Steiner. The festival for 1914 with a projected fifth mystery drama was cancelled because of the outbreak of the First World War.

Page 128, "our various kinds of hardwood..."
Compare this with the lecture of June 29, 1921, in CW 290.

Page 128, "a person came to us as a friend..."
Maria Strauch-Spettini (1847–1904). Actress at the Dresden Court Theater, then at the German Imperial Theater in St. Petersburg; retired into private life in 1883. From 1897 on teacher and friend of Marie Steiner, then Marie von Sivers. See *From the Life of Marie Steiner-von Sivers*, Dornach 1956.

Page 129, "myself and two others."
Rudolf Steiner, Marie Steiner, then von Sivers, and Maria von Strauch-Spettini. Compare above.

Page 129, "at our congress..."
See CW 284/285.

RUDOLF STEINER'S COLLECTED WORKS

The German Edition of Rudolf Steiner's Collected Works (the *Gesamtausgabe* [GA] published by Rudolf Steiner Verlag, Dornach, Switzerland) presently runs to over 354 titles, organized either by type of work (written or spoken), chronology, audience (public or other), or subject (education, art, etc.). For ease of comparison, the Collected Works in English [CW] follows the German organization. A complete listing of the CWs follows with the *literal translations* of the German titles. Other than in the case of the books published in his lifetime, titles were rarely given by Rudolf Steiner himself, and were often provided by the editors of the German editions. The titles in English are not necessarily the same as the German; and, indeed, over the past seventy-five years have frequently bee different, with the same book sometimes appearing under different titles.

For ease of identification and to avoid confusion, we suggest that readers looking for a title should do so by CW number. Because the work of creating the Collected Works of Rudolf Steiner is an ongoing process, with new titles being published every year, we have not indicated in this listing which books are presently available. To find out what titles in the Collected Works are currently in print, please check our website at www.steinerbooks.org.

Written Work

CW 1	Goethe: Natural-Scientific Writings, Introduction, with Footnotes and Explanations in the text by Rudolf Steiner
CW 2	Outlines of an Epistemology of the Goethean World View, with Special Consideration of Schiller
CW 3	Truth and Science
CW 4	The Philosophy of Freedom
CW 4a	Documents to "The Philosophy of Freedom"
CW 5	Friedrich Nietzsche, A Fighter against His Own Time
CW 6	Goethe's Worldview
CW 6a	Now in CW 30
CW 7	Mysticism at the Dawn of Modern Spiritual Life and Its Relationship with Modern Worldviews
CW 8	Christianity as Mystical Fact and the Mysteries of Antiquity
CW 9	Theosophy: An Introduction into Supersensible World Knowledge and Human Purpose
CW 10	How Does One Attain Knowledge of Higher Worlds?
CW 11	From the Akasha-Chronicle
CW 12	Levels of Higher Knowledge

CW 13 Occult Science in Outline
CW 14 Four Mystery Dramas
CW 15 The Spiritual Guidance of the Individual and Humanity
CW 16 A Way to Human Self-Knowledge: Eight Meditations
CW 17 The Threshold of the Spiritual World. Aphoristic Comments
CW 18 The Riddles of Philosophy in Their History, Presented as an Outline
CW 19 Contained in CW 24
CW 20 The Riddles of the Human Being: Articulated and Unarticulated in the Thinking, Views and Opinions of a Series of German and Austrian Personalities
CW 21 The Riddles of the Soul
CW 22 Goethe's Spiritual Nature And Its Revelation In "Faust" and through the "Fairy Tale of the Snake and the Lily"
CW 23 The Central Points of the Social Question in the Necessities of Life in the Present and the Future
CW 24 Essays Concerning the Threefold Division of the Social Organism and the Period 1915-1921
CW 25 Cosmology, Religion and Philosophy
CW 26 Anthroposophical Leading Thoughts
CW 27 Fundamentals for Expansion of the Art of Healing according to Spiritual-Scientific Insights
CW 28 The Course of My Life
CW 29 Collected Essays on Dramaturgy, 1889-1900
CW 30 Methodical Foundations of Anthroposophy: Collected Essays on Philosophy, Natural Science, Aesthetics and Psychology, 1884-1901
CW 31 Collected Essays on Culture and Current Events, 1887-1901
CW 32 Collected Essays on Literature, 1884-1902
CW 33 Biographies and Biographical Sketches, 1894-1905
CW 34 Lucifer-Gnosis: Foundational Essays on Anthroposophy and Reports from the Periodicals "Lucifer" and "Lucifer-Gnosis," 1903-1908
CW 35 Philosophy and Anthroposophy: Collected Essays, 1904-1923
CW 36 The Goetheanum-Idea in the Middle of the Cultural Crisis of the Present: Collected Essays from the Periodical "Das Goetheanum," 1921-1925
CW 37 Now in CWs 260a and 251
CW 38 Letters, Vol. 1: 1881-1890
CW 39 Letters, Vol. 2: 1890-1925
CW 40 Truth-Wrought Words
CW 40a Sayings, Poems and Mantras; Supplementary Volume
CW 42 Now in CWs 264-266

CW 43 Stage Adaptations
CW 44 On the Four Mystery Dramas. Sketches, Fragments and Paralipomena on the Four Mystery Dramas
CW 45 Anthroposophy: A Fragment from the Year 1910

Public Lectures

CW 51 On Philosophy, History and Literature
CW 52 Spiritual Teachings Concerning the Soul and Observation of the World
CW 53 The Origin and Goal of the Human Being
CW 54 The Riddles of the World and Anthroposophy
CW 55 Knowledge of the Supersensible in Our Times and Its Meaning for Life Today
CW 56 Knowledge of the Soul and of the Spirit
CW 57 Where and How Does One Find the Spirit?
CW 58 The Metamorphoses of the Soul Life. Paths of Soul Experiences: Part One
CW 59 The Metamorphoses of the Soul Life. Paths of Soul Experiences: Part Two
CW 60 The Answers of Spiritual Science to the Biggest Questions of Existence
CW 61 Human History in the Light of Spiritual Research
CW 62 Results of Spiritual Research
CW 63 Spiritual Science as a Treasure for Life
CW 64 Out of Destiny-Burdened Times
CW 65 Out of Central European Spiritual Life
CW 66 Spirit and Matter, Life and Death
CW 67 The Eternal in the Human Soul. Immortality and Freedom
CW 68 Public lectures in various cities, 1906-1918
CW 69 Public lectures in various cities, 1906-1918
CW 70 Public lectures in various cities, 1906-1918
CW 71 Public lectures in various cities, 1906-1918
CW 72 Freedom – Immortality – Social Life
CW 73 The Supplementing of the Modern Sciences through Anthroposophy
CW 73a Specialized Fields of Knowledge and Anthroposophy
CW 74 The Philosophy of Thomas Aquinas
CW 75 Public lectures in various cities, 1906-1918
CW 76 The Fructifying Effect of Anthroposophy on Specialized Fields
CW 77a The Task of Anthroposophy in Relation to Science and Life: The Darmstadt College Course

CW 77b	Art and Anthroposophy. The Goetheanum-Impulse
CW 78	Anthroposophy, Its Roots of Knowledge and Fruits for Life
CW 79	The Reality of the Higher Worlds
CW 80	Public Lectures in Various Cities, 1922
CW 81	Renewal-Impulses for Culture and Science – Berlin College Course
CW 82	So that the Human Being Can Become a Complete Human Being
CW 83	Western and Eastern World-Contrast. Paths to Understanding It through Anthroposophy
CW 84	What Did the Goetheanum Intend and What Should Anthroposophy Do?

Lectures to the Members of the Anthroposophical Society

CW 88	Concerning the Astral World and Devachan
CW 89	Consciousness – Life – Form. Fundamental Principles of a Spiritual-Scientific Cosmology
CW 90	Participant Notes from the Lectures during the Years 1903-1905
CW 91	Participant Notes from the Lectures during the Years 1903-1905
CW 92	The Occult Truths of Ancient Myths and Sagas
CW 93	The Temple Legend and the Golden Legend
CW 93a	Fundamentals of Esotericism
CW 94	Cosmogony. Popular Occultism. The Gospel of John. The Theosophy in the Gospel of John
CW 95	At the Gates of Theosophy
CW 96	Origin-Impulses of Spiritual Science. Christian Esotericism in the Light of New Spirit-Knowledge
CW 97	The Christian Mystery
CW 98	Nature Beings and Spirit Beings – Their Effects in Our Visible World
CW 99	The Theosophy of the Rosicrucians
CW 100	Human Development and Christ-Knowledge
CW 101	Myths and Legends. Occult Signs and Symbols
CW 102	The Working into Human Beings by Spiritual Beings
CW 103	The Gospel of John
CW 104	The Apocalypse of John
CW 104a	From the Picture-Script of the Apocalypse of John
CW 105	Universe, Earth, the Human Being: Their Being and Development, as well as Their Reflection in the Connection between Egyptian Mythology and Modern Culture
CW 106	Egyptian Myths and Mysteries in Relation to the active Spiritual Forces of the Present

CW 107	Spiritual-Scientific Knowledge of the Human Being
CW 108	Answering the Questions of Life and the World through Anthroposophy
CW 109	The Principle of Spiritual Economy in Connection with the Question of Reincarnation. An Aspect of the Spiritual Guidance of Humanity
CW 110	The Spiritual Hierarchies and their Reflection in the Physical World. Zodiac, Planets and Cosmos
CW 111	Contained in 109
CW 112	The Gospel of John in Relation to the Three Other Gospels, Especially the Gospel of Luke
CW 113	The Orient in the Light of the Occident. The Children of Lucifer and the Brothers of Christ
CW 114	The Gospel of Luke
CW 115	Anthroposophy – Psychosophy – Pneumatosophy
CW 116	The Christ-Impulse and the Development of "I"-Consciousness
CW 117	The Deeper Secrets of the Development of Humanity in Light of the Gospels
CW 118	The Event of the Christ-Appearance in the Etheric World
CW 119	Macrocosm and Microcosm. The Large World and the Small World. Soul-Questions, Life-Questions, Spirit-Questions
CW 120	The Revelation of Karma
CW 121	The Mission of Individual Folk-Souls in Connection with Germanic-Nordic Mythology
CW 122	The Secrets of the Biblical Creation-Story. The Six-Day Work in the First Book of Moses
CW 123	The Gospel of Matthew
CW 124	Excursus in the Area of the Gospel of Mark
CW 125	Paths and Goals of the Spiritual Human Being. Life Questions in the Light of Spiritual Science
CW 126	Occult History. Esoteric Observations of the Karmic Relationships of Personalities and Events of World History
CW 127	The Mission of the New Spiritual Revelation. The Christ-Event as the Middle-Point of Earth Evolution
CW 128	An Occult Physiology
CW 129	Wonders of the World, Trials of the Soul, and Revelations of the Spirit
CW 130	Esoteric Christianity and the Spiritual Guidance of Humanity
CW 131	From Jesus to Christ
CW 132	Evolution from the View Point of the Truth
CW 133	The Earthly and the Cosmic Human Being
CW 134	The World of the Senses and the World of the Spirit

CW 135	Reincarnation and Karma and their Meaning for the Culture of the Present
CW 136	The Spiritual Beings in Celestial Bodies and the Realms of Nature
CW 137	The Human Being in the Light of Occultism, Theosophy and Philosophy
CW 138	On Initiation. On Eternity and the Passing Moment. On the Light of the Spirit and the Darkness of Life
CW 139	The Gospel of Mark
CW 140	Occult Investigation into the Life Between Death and New Birth. The Living Interaction Between Life and Death
CW 141	Life Between Death and New Birth in Relationship to Cosmic Facts
CW 142	The Bhagavad-Gita and the Letters of Paul
CW 143	Experiences of the Supersensible. Three Paths of the Soul to Christ
CW 144	The Mysteries of the East and of Christianity
CW 145	What Significance Does Occult Development of the Human Being Have for His Sheaths – Physical Body, Etheric Body, Astral Body, and Self?
CW 146	The Occult Foundations of the Bhagavad-Gita
CW 147	The Secrets of the Threshold
CW 148	Out of Research in the Akasha: The Fifth Gospel
CW 149	Christ and the Spiritual World. Concerning the Search for the Holy Grail
CW 150	The World of the Spirit and Its Extension into Physical Existence. The Influence of the Dead in the World of the Living
CW 151	Human Thought and Cosmic Thought
CW 152	Preliminary Stages to the Mystery of Golgotha
CW 153	The Inner Being of the Human Being and Life Between Death and New Birth
CW 154	How does One Gain an Understanding of the Spiritual World? The Flowing in of Spiritual Impulses from out of the World of the Deceased
CW 155	Christ and the Human Soul. Concerning the Meaning of Life. Theosophical Morality. Anthroposophy and Christianity
CW 156	Occult Reading and Occult Hearing
CW 157	Human Destinies and the Destiny of Peoples
CW 157a	The Formation of Destiny and the Life After Death
CW 158	The Connection Between the Human Being and the Elemental World. Kalevala – Olaf Asteson – The Russian People – The World as the Result of the Influences of Equilibrium
CW 159	The Mystery of Death. The Nature and Significance of Middle Europe and the European Folk Spirits
CW 160	In CW 159

CW 161	Paths of Spiritual Knowledge and the Renewal of the Artistic Worldview
CW 162	Questions of Art and Life in Light of Spiritual Science
CW 163	Coincidence, Necessity and Providence. Imaginative Knowledge and the Processes after Death
CW 164	The Value of Thinking for a Knowledge that Satisfies the Human Being. The Relationship of Spiritual Science to Natural Science.
CW 165	The Spiritual Unification of Humanity through the Christ-Impulse
CW 166	Necessity and Freedom in the Events of the World and in Human Action
CW 167	The Present and the Past in the Human Spirit
CW 168	The Connection between the Living and the Dead
CW 169	World-being and Selfhood
CW 170	The Riddle of the Human Being. The Spiritual Background of Human History. Cosmic and Human History, Vol. 1
CW 171	Inner Development-Impulses of Humanity. Goethe and the Crisis of the 19th Century. Cosmic and Human History, Vol. 2
CW 172	The Karma of the Vocation of the Human Being in Connection with Goethe's Life. Cosmic and Human History, Vol. 3
CW 173	Contemporary-Historical Considerations: The Karma of Untruthfulness, Part One. Cosmic and Human History, Vol. 4
CW 174	Contemporary-Historical Considerations: The Karma of Untruthfulness, Part Two. Cosmic and Human History, Vol. 5
CW 174a	Middle Europe Between East and West. Cosmic and Human History, Vol. 6
CW 174b	The Spiritual Background of the First World War. Cosmic and Human History, Vol. 7
CW 175	Building Stones for an Understanding of the Mystery of Golgotha. Cosmic and Human Metamorphoses.
CW 176	Truths of Evolution of the Individual and Humanity. The Karma of Materialism
CW 177	The Spiritual Background of the Outer World. The Fall of the Spirits of Darkness. Spiritual Beings and Their Effects, Vol. 1
CW 178	Individual Spiritual Beings and their Influence in the Soul of the Human Being. Spiritual Beings and their Effects, Vol. 2
CW 179	Spiritual Beings and Their Effects. Historical Necessity and Freedom. The Influences on Destiny from out of the World of the Dead. Spiritual Beings and Their Effects, Vol. 3
CW 180	Mystery Truths and Christmas Impulses. Ancient Myths and their Meaning. Spiritual Beings and Their Effects, Vol. 4
CW 181	Earthly Death and Cosmic Life. Anthroposophical Gifts for Life. Necessities of Consciousness for the Present and the Future
CW 182	Death as Transformation of Life
CW 183	The Science of the Development of the Human Being

CW 184	The Polarity of Duration and Development in Human Life. The Cosmic Pre-History of Humanity
CW 185	Historical Symptomology
CW 185a	Historical-Developmental Foundations for Forming a Social Judgment
CW 186	The Fundamental Social Demands of Our Time–In Changed Situations
CW 187	How Can Humanity Find the Christ Again? The Threefold Shadow-Existence of our Time and the New Christ-Light
CW 188	Goetheanism, a Transformation-Impulse and Resurrection-Thought. Science of the Human Being and Science of Sociology
CW 189	The Social Question as a Question of Consciousness. The Spiritual Background of the Social Question, Vol. 1
CW 190	Impulses of the Past and the Future in Social Occurrences. The Spiritual Background of the Social Question, Vol. 2
CW 191	Social Understanding from Spiritual-Scientific Cognition. The Spiritual Background of the Social Question, Vol. 3
CW 192	Spiritual-Scientific Treatment of Social and Pedagogical Questions
CW 193	The Inner Aspect of the Social Riddle. Luciferic Past and Ahrimanic Future
CW 194	The Mission of Michael. The Revelation of the Actual Mysteries of the Human Being
CW 195	Cosmic New Year and the New Year Idea
CW 196	Spiritual and Social Transformations in the Development of Humanity
CW 197	Polarities in the Development of Humanity: West and East-Materialism and Mysticism-Knowledge and Belief
CW 198	Healing Factors for the Social Organism
CW 199	Spiritual Science as Knowledge of the Foundational Impulses of Social Formation
CW 200	The New Spirituality and the Christ-Experience of the 20th Century
CW 201	The Correspondences Between Microcosm and Macrocosm. The Human Being – A Hieroglyph of the Universe. The Human Being in Relationship with the Cosmos: 1
CW 202	The Bridge between the World-Spirituality and the Physical Aspect of the Human Being. The Search for the New Isis, the Divine Sophia. The Human Being in Relationship with the Cosmos: 2
CW 203	The Responsibility of Human Beings for the Development of the World through their Spiritual Connection with the Planet Earth and the World of the Stars. The Human Being in Relationship with the Cosmos: 3
CW 204	Perspectives of the Development of Humanity. The Materialistic Knowledge-Impulse and the Task of Anthroposophy. The Human Being in Relationship with the Cosmos: 4

CW 205	Human Development, World-Soul, and World-Spirit. Part One: The Human Being as a Being of Body and Soul in His Relationship to the World. The Human Being in Relationship with the Cosmos: 5
CW 206	Human Development, World-Soul, and World-Spirit. Part Two: The Human Being as a Spiritual Being in the process of Historical Development. The Human Being in Relationship with the Cosmos: 6
CW 207	Anthroposophy as Cosmosophy. Part One: Characteristic Features of the Human Being in the Earthly and the Cosmic Realms. The Human Being in Relationship with the Cosmos: 7
CW 208	Anthroposophy as Cosmosophy. Part Two: The Forming of the Human Being as the Result of Cosmic Influence. The Human Being in Relationship with the Cosmos: 8
CW 209	Nordic and Central European Spiritual Impulses. The Festival of the Appearance of Christ. The Human Being in Relationship with the Cosmos: 9
CW 210	Old and New Methods of Initiation. Drama and Poetry in the Change of Consciousness in the Modern Age
CW 211	The Sun Mystery and the Mystery of Death and Resurrection. Exoteric and Esoteric Christianity
CW 212	Human Soul Life and Spiritual Striving in Connection with World and Earth Development
CW 213	Human Questions and World Answers
CW 214	The Mystery of the Trinity: The Human Being and His Relationship to the Spiritual World in the Course of Time
CW 215	Philosophy, Cosmology, and Religion in Anthroposophy
CW 216	The Fundamental Impulses of the World-Historical Development of Humanity
CW 217	Spiritually Active Forces in the Coexistence of the Older and Younger Generations. Pedagogical Course for Youth
CW 217a	Youth's Cognitive Task
CW 218	Spiritual Connections in the Forming of the Human Organism
CW 219	The Relationship of the World of the Stars to the Human Being, and of the Human Being to the World of the Stars. The Spiritual Communion of Humanity
CW 220	Living Knowledge of Nature. Intellectual Fall and Spiritual Redemption
CW 221	Earth-Knowing and Heaven-Insight
CW 222	The Imparting of Impulses to World-Historical Events through Spiritual Powers
CW 223	The Cycle of the Year as Breathing Process of the Earth and the Four Great Festival-Seasons. Anthroposophy and the Human Heart

CW 224	The Human Soul and its Connection with Divine-Spiritual Individualities. The Internalization of the Festivals of the Year
CW 225	Three Perspectives of Anthroposophy. Cultural Phenomena observed from a Spiritual-Scientific Perspective
CW 226	Human Being, Human Destiny, and World Development
CW 227	Initiation-Knowledge
CW 228	Science of Initiation and Knowledge of the Stars. The Human Being in the Past, the Present, and the Future from the Viewpoint of the Development of Consciousness
CW 229	The Experiencing of the Course of the Year in Four Cosmic Imaginations
CW 230	The Human Being as Harmony of the Creative, Building, and Formative World-Word
CW 231	The Supersensible Human Being, Understood Anthroposophically
CW 232	The Forming of the Mysteries
CW 233	World History Illuminated by Anthroposophy and as the Foundation for Knowledge of the Human Spirit
CW 233a	Mystery Sites of the Middle Ages: Rosicrucianism and the Modern Initiation-Principle. The Festival of Easter as Part of the History of the Mysteries of Humanity
CW 234	Anthroposophy. A Summary after 21 Years
CW 235	Esoteric Observations of Karmic Relationships in 6 Volumes, Vol. 1
CW 236	Esoteric Observations of Karmic Relationships in 6 Volumes, Vol. 2
CW 237	Esoteric Observations of Karmic Relationships in 6 Volumes, Vol. 3. The Karmic Relationships of the Anthroposophical Movement
CW 238	Esoteric Observations of Karmic Relationships in 6 Volumes, Vol. 4: The Spiritual Life of the Present in Relationship to the Anthroposophical Movement
CW 239	Esoteric Observations of Karmic Relationships in 6 Volumes, Vol. 5
CW 240	Esoteric Observations of Karmic Relationships in 6 Volumes, Vol. 6
CW 243	The Consciousness of the Initiate
CW 245	Instructions for an Esoteric Schooling
CW 250	The Building-Up of the Anthroposophical Society. From the Beginning to the Outbreak of the First World War
CW 251	The History of the Goetheanum Building-Association
CW 252	Life in the Anthroposophical Society from the First World War to the Burning of the First Goetheanum
CW 253	The Problems of Living Together in the Anthroposophical Society. On the Dornach Crisis of 1915. With Highlights on Swedenborg's Clairvoyance, the Views of Freudian Psychoanalysts, and the Concept of Love in Relation to Mysticism

CW 254	The Occult Movement in the 19th Century and Its Relationship to World Culture. Significant Points from the exoteric Cultural Life around the Middle of the 19th Century
CW 255	Rudolf Steiner during the First World War
CW 255a	Anthroposophy and the Reformation of Society. On the History of the Threefold Movement
CW 255b	Anthroposophy and Its Opponents, 1919-1921
CW 256	How Can the Anthroposophical Movement Be Financed?
CW 256a	Futurum, Inc. / International Laboratories, Inc.
CW 256b	The Coming Day, Inc.
CW 257	Anthroposophical Community-Building
CW 258	The History of and Conditions for the Anthroposophical Movement in Relationship to the Anthroposophical Society. A Stimulus to Self-Contemplation
CW 259	The Year of Destiny 1923 in the History of the Anthroposophical Society. From the Burning of the Goetheanum to the Christmas Conference
CW 260	The Christmas Conference for the Founding of the General Anthroposophical Society
CW 260a	The Constitution of the General Anthroposophical Society and the School for Spiritual Science. The Rebuilding of the Goetheanum
CW 261	Our Dead. Addresses, Words of Remembrance, and Meditative Verses, 1906-1924
CW 262	Rudolf Steiner and Marie Steiner-von Sivers: Correspondence and Documents, 1901-1925
CW 263/1	Rudolf Steiner and Edith Maryon: Correspondence: Letters, Verses, Sketches, 1912-1924
CW 264	On the History and the Contents of the First Section of the Esoteric School from 1904 to 1914. Letters, Newsletters, Documents, Lectures
CW 265	On the History and Out of the Contents of the Ritual-Knowledge Section of the Esoteric School from 1904 to 1914. Documents, and Lectures from the Years 1906 to 1914, as well as on New Approaches to Ritual-Knowledge Work in the Years 1921-1924
CW 266/1	From the Contents of the Esoteric Lessons. Volume 1: 1904-1909. Notes from Memory of Participants. Meditation texts from the notes of Rudolf Steiner
CW 266/2	From the Contents of the Esoteric Lessons. Volume 2: 1910-1912. Notes from Memory of Participants
CW 266/3	From the Contents of the Esoteric Lessons. Volume 3: 1913, 1914 and 1920-1923. Notes from Memory of Participants. Meditation texts from the notes of Rudolf Steiner

CW 267 Soul-Exercises: Vol. 1: Exercises with Word and Image Meditations for the Methodological Development of Higher Powers of Knowledge, 1904-1924
CW 268 Soul-Exercises: Vol. 2: Mantric Verses, 1903-1925
CW 269 Ritual Texts for the Celebration of the Free Christian Religious Instruction. The Collected Verses for Teachers and Students of the Waldorf School
CW 270 Esoteric Instructions for the First Class of the School for Spiritual Science at the Goetheanum 1924, 4 Volumes
CW 271 Art and Knowledge of Art. Foundations of a New Aesthetic
CW 272 Spiritual-Scientific Commentary on Goethe's "Faust" in Two Volumes. Vol. 1: Faust, the Striving Human Being
CW 273 Spiritual-Scientific Commentary on Goethe's "Faust" in Two Volumes. Vol. 2: The Faust-Problem
CW 274 Addresses for the Christmas Plays from the Old Folk Traditions
CW 275 Art in the Light of Mystery-Wisdom
CW 276 The Artistic in Its Mission in the World. The Genius of Language. The World of the Self-Revealing Radiant Appearances – Anthroposophy and Art. Anthroposophy and Poetry
CW 277 Eurythmy. The Revelation of the Speaking Soul
CW 277a The Origin and Development of Eurythmy
CW 278 Eurythmy as Visible Song
CW 279 Eurythmy as Visible Speech
CW 280 The Method and Nature of Speech Formation
CW 281 The Art of Recitation and Declamation
CW 282 Speech Formation and Dramatic Art
CW 283 The Nature of Things Musical and the Experience of Tone in the Human Being
CW284/285 Images of Occult Seals and Pillars. The Munich Congress of Whitsun 1907 and Its Consequences
CW 286 Paths to a New Style of Architecture. "And the Building Becomes Human"
CW 287 The Building at Dornach as a Symbol of Historical Becoming and an Artistic Transformation Impulses
CW 288 Style-Forms in the Living Organic
CW 289 The Building-Idea of the Goetheanum: Lectures with Slides from the Years 1920-1921
CW 290 The Building-Idea of the Goetheanum: Lectures with Slides from the Years 1920-1921
CW 291 The Nature of Colors

CW 291a	Knowledge of Colors. Supplementary Volume to "The Nature of Colors"
CW 292	Art History as Image of Inner Spiritual Impulses
CW 293	General Knowledge of the Human Being as the Foundation of Pedagogy
CW 294	The Art of Education, Methodology and Didactics
CW 295	The Art of Education: Seminar Discussions and Lectures on Lesson Planning
CW 296	The Question of Education as a Social Question
CW 297	The Idea and Practice of the Waldorf School
CW 297a	Education for Life: Self-Education and the Practice of Pedagogy
CW 298	Rudolf Steiner in the Waldorf School
CW 299	Spiritual-Scientific Observations on Speech
CW 300a	Conferences with the Teachers of the Free Waldorf School in Stuttgart, 1919 to 1924, in 3 Volumes. Vol.1
CW 300b	Conferences with the Teachers of the Free Waldorf School in Stuttgart, 1919 to 1924, in 3 Volumes. Vol. 2
CW 300c	Conferences with the Teachers of the Free Waldorf School in Stuttgart, 1919 to 1924, in 3 Volumes. Vol. 3
CW 301	The Renewal of the Pedagogical-Didactical Art through Spiritual Science
CW 302	Knowledge of the Human Being and the Forming of Class Lessons
CW 302a	Education and Teaching out of a Knowledge of the Human Being
CW 303	The Healthy Development of the Human Being
CW 304	Methods of Education and Teaching Based on Anthroposophy
CW 304a	Anthroposophical Knowledge of the Human Being and Pedagogy
CW 305	The Soul-Spiritual Foundational Forces of the Art of Education. Spiritual Values in Education and Social Life
CW 306	Pedagogical Praxis from the Viewpoint of a Spiritual-Scientific Knowledge of the Human Being. The Education of the Child and Young Human Beings
CW 307	The Spiritual Life of the Present and Education
CW 308	The Method of Teaching and the Life-Requirements for Teaching
CW 309	Anthroposophical Pedagogy and Its Prerequisites
CW 310	The Pedagogical Value of a Knowledge of the Human Being and the Cultural Value of Pedagogy
CW 311	The Art of Education Out of an Understanding of the Being of Humanity
CW 312	Spiritual Science and Medicine
CW 313	Spiritual-Scientific Viewpoints on Therapy
CW 314	Physiology and Therapy Based on Spiritual Science
CW 315	Curative Eurythmy

CW 316 Meditative Observations and Instructions for a Deepening of the Art of Healing
CW 317 The Curative Education Course
CW 318 The Working Together of Doctors and Pastors
CW 319 Anthroposophical Knowledge of the Human Being and Medicine
CW 320 Spiritual-Scientific Impulses for the Development of Physics 1: The First Natural-Scientific Course: Light, Color, Tone, Mass, Electricity, Magnetism
CW 321 Spiritual-Scientific Impulses for the Development of Physics 2: The Second Natural-Scientific Course: Warmth at the Border of the Positive and Negative materiality
CW 322 The Borders of the Knowledge of Nature
CW 323 The Relationship of the various Natural-Scientific Fields to Astronomy
CW 324 Nature Observation, Mathematics, and Scientific Experimentation and Results from the Viewpoint of Anthroposophy
CW 324a The Fourth Dimension in Mathematics and Reality
CW 325 Natural Science and the World-Historical Development of Humanity since Ancient Times
CW 326 The Moment of the Coming into Being of Natural Science in World History and its Development since Then
CW 327 Spiritual-Scientific Foundations for Success in Farming. The Agricultural Course
CW 328 The Social Question
CW 329 The Liberation of the Human Being as the Foundation for a New Social Form
CW 330 The Renewal of the Social Organism
CW 331 Work-Council and Socialization
CW 332 The Alliance for Threefolding and the Total Reform of Society. The Council on Culture and the Liberation of the Spiritual Life
CW 332a The Social Future
CW 333 Freedom of Thought and Social Forces
CW 334 From the Unified State to the Threefold Social Organism
CW 335 The Crisis of the Present and the Path to Healthy Thinking
CW 336 The Great Questions of the Times and Anthroposophical Spiritual Knowledge
CW 337a Social Ideas, Social Reality, Social Practice, Vol. 1: Question-and-Answer Evenings and Study Evenings of the Alliance for the Threefold Social Organism in Stuttgart, 1919-1920
CW 337b Social Ideas, Social Realities, Social Practice, Vol. 2: Discussion Evenings of the Swiss Alliance for the Threefold Social Organism

CW 338 How Does One Work on Behalf of the Impulse for the Threefold Social Organism?

CW 339 Anthroposophy, Threefold Social Organism, and the Art of Public Speaking

CW 340 The National-Economics Course. The Tasks of a New Science of Economics, Volume 1

CW 341 The National-Economics Seminar. The Tasks of a New Science of Economics, Volume 2

CW 342 Lectures and Courses on Christian Religious Work. Vol.1: Anthroposophical Foundations for a Renewed Christian Religious Working

CW 343 Lectures and Courses on Christian Religious Work. Vol. 2: Spiritual Knowledge – Religious Feeling – Cultic Doing

CW 344 Lectures and Courses on Christian Religious Work. Vol. 3: Lectures at the Founding of the Christian Community

CW 345 Lectures and Courses on Christian Religious Work. Vol. 4: Concerning the Nature of the Working Word

CW 346 Lectures and Courses on Christian Religious Work. Vol. 5: The Apocalypse and the Working of the Priest

CW 347 The Knowledge of the Nature of the Human Being According to Body, Soul and Spirit. On Earlier Conditions of the Earth

CW 348 On Health and Illness. Foundations of a Spiritual-Scientific Doctrine of the Senses

CW 349 On the Life of Human Being and of the Earth. On the Nature of Christianity

CW 350 Rhythms in the Cosmos and in the Human Being. How Does One Come To See the Spiritual World?

CW 351 The Human Being and the World. The Influence of the Spirit in Nature. On the Nature of Bees

CW 352 Nature and the Human Being Observed Spiritual-Scientifically

CW 353 The History of Humanity and the World-Views of the Folk Cultures

CW 354 The Creation of the World and the Human Being. Life on Earth and the Influence of the Stars

SIGNIFICANT EVENTS IN THE LIFE OF RUDOLF STEINER

1829: June 23: birth of Johann Steiner (1829-1910)—Rudolf Steiner's father—in Geras, Lower Austria.

1834: May 8: birth of Franciska Blie (1834-1918)—Rudolf Steiner's mother—in Horn, Lower Austria. "My father and mother were both children of the glorious Lower Austrian forest district north of the Danube."

1860: May 16: marriage of Johann Steiner and Franciska Blie.

1861: February 25: birth of *Rudolf Joseph Lorenz Steiner* in Kraljevec, Croatia, near the border with Hungary, where Johann Steiner works as a telegrapher for the South Austria Railroad. Rudolf Steiner is baptized two days later, February 27, the date usually given as his birthday.

1862: Summer: the family moves to Mödling, Lower Austria.

1863: The family moves to Pottschach, Lower Austria, near the Styrian border, where Johann Steiner becomes stationmaster. "The view stretched to the mountains...majestic peaks in the distance and the sweet charm of nature in the immediate surroundings."

1864: November 15: birth of Rudolf Steiner's sister, Leopoldine (d. November 1, 1927). She will become a seamstress and live with her parents for the rest of her life.

1866: July 28: birth of Rudolf Steiner's deaf-mute brother, Gustav (d. May 1, 1941).

1867: Rudolf Steiner enters the village school. Following a disagreement between his father and the schoolmaster, whose wife falsely accused the boy of causing a commotion, Rudolf Steiner is taken out of school and taught at home.

1868: A critical experience. Unknown to the family, an aunt dies in a distant town. Sitting in the station waiting room, Rudolf Steiner sees her "form," which speaks to him, asking for help. "Beginning with this experience, a new soul life began in the boy, one in which not only the outer trees and mountains spoke to him, but also the worlds that lay behind them. From this moment on, the boy began to live with the spirits of nature...."

1869: The family moves to the peaceful, rural village of Neudorfl, near Wiener-Neustadt in present-day Austria. Rudolf Steiner attends the village school. Because of the "unorthodoxy" of his writing and spelling, he has to do "extra lessons."

1870: Through a book lent to him by his tutor, he discovers geometry: "To grasp something purely in the spirit brought me inner happiness. I know that I first learned happiness through geometry." The same tutor allows him to draw, while other students still struggle with their reading and writing. "An artistic element" thus enters his education.

1871: Though his parents are not religious, Rudolf Steiner becomes a "church child," a favorite of the priest, who was "an exceptional character." "Up to the age of ten or eleven, among those I came to know, he was far and away the most significant." Among other things, he introduces Steiner to Copernican, heliocentric cosmology. As an altar boy, Rudolf Steiner serves at Masses, funerals, and Corpus Christi processions. At year's end, after an incident in which he escapes a thrashing, his father forbids him to go to church.

1872: Rudolf Steiner transfers to grammar school in Wiener-Neustadt, a five-mile walk from home, which must be done in all weathers.

1873-75: Through his teachers and on his own, Rudolf Steiner has many wonderful experiences with science and mathematics. Outside school, he teaches himself analytic geometry, trigonometry, differential equations, and calculus.

1876: Rudolf Steiner begins tutoring other students. He learns bookbinding from his father. He also teaches himself stenography.

1877: Rudolf Steiner discovers Kant's *Critique of Pure Reason*, which he reads and rereads. He also discovers and reads von Rotteck's *World History*.

1878: He studies extensively in contemporary psychology and philosophy.

1879: Rudolf Steiner graduates from high school with honors. His father is transferred to Inzersdorf, near Vienna. He uses his first visit to Vienna "to purchase a great number of philosophy books"—Kant, Fichte, Schelling, and Hegel, as well as numerous histories of philosophy. His aim: to find a path from the "I" to nature.

October 1879-1883: Rudolf Steiner attends the Technical College in Vienna—to study mathematics, chemistry, physics, mineralogy, botany, zoology, biology, geology, and mechanics—with a scholarship. He also attends lectures in history and literature, while avidly reading philosophy on his own. His two favorite professors are Karl Julius Schröer (German language and literature) and Edmund Reitlinger (physics). He also audits lectures by Robert Zimmerman on aesthetics and Franz Brentano on philosophy. During this year he begins his friendship with Moritz Zitter (1861-1921), who will help support him financially when he is in Berlin.

1880: Rudolf Steiner attends lectures on Schiller and Goethe by Karl Julius Schröer, who becomes his mentor. Also "through a remarkable combination of circumstances," he meets Felix Koguzki, an "herb gatherer" and healer, who could "see deeply into the secrets of nature." Rudolf Steiner will meet and study with this "emissary of the Master" throughout his time in Vienna.

1881: January: "... I didn't sleep a wink. I was busy with philosophical problems until about 12:30 a.m. Then, finally, I threw myself down on my couch. All my striving during the previous year had been to research whether the following statement by Schelling was true or not: *Within everyone dwells a secret, marvelous capacity to draw back from the stream of time—out of the self clothed in all that comes to us from outside—into our innermost being and there, in the immutable form of the Eternal, to look into ourselves.* I believe, and I am still quite certain of it, that I discovered this capacity in myself; I had long had an inkling of it. Now the whole of idealist philosophy stood before me in modified form. What's a sleepless night compared to that!"

Rudolf Steiner begins communicating with leading thinkers of the day, who send him books in return, which he reads eagerly.

July: "I am not one of those who dives into the day like an animal in human form. I pursue a quite specific goal, an idealistic aim—knowledge of the truth! This cannot be done offhandedly. It requires the greatest striving in the world, free of all egotism, and equally of all resignation."

August: Steiner puts down on paper for the first time thoughts for a "Philosophy of Freedom." "The striving for the absolute: this human yearning is freedom." He also seeks to outline a "peasant philosophy," describing what the worldview of a "peasant"—one who lives close to the earth and the old ways—really is.

1881-1882: Felix Koguzki, the herb gatherer, reveals himself to be the envoy of another, higher initiatory personality, who instructs Rudolf Steiner to penetrate Fichte's philosophy and to master modern scientific thinking as a preparation for right entry into the spirit. This "Master" also teaches him the double (evolutionary and involutionary) nature of time.

1882: Through the offices of Karl Julius Schröer, Rudolf Steiner is asked by Joseph Kurschner to edit Goethe's scientific works for the *Deutschen National-Literatur* edition. He writes "A Possible Critique of Atomistic Concepts" and sends it to Friedrich Theodore Vischer.

1883: Rudolf Steiner completes his college studies and begins work on the Goethe project.

1884: First volume of Goethe's *Scientific Writings* (CW 1) appears (March). He lectures on Goethe and Lessing, and Goethe's approach to science. In July, he enters the household of Ladislaus and Pauline Specht as tutor to the four Specht boys. He will live there until 1890. At this time, he meets Josef Breuer ((1842-1925), the coauthor with Sigmund Freud of *Studies in Hysteria*, who is the Specht family doctor.

1885: While continuing to edit Goethe's writings, Rudolf Steiner reads deeply in contemporary philosophy (Edouard von Hartmann, Johannes Volkelt, and Richard Wahle, among others).

1886: May: Rudolf Steiner sends Kurschner the manuscript of *Outlines of Goethe's Theory of Knowledge* (CW 2), which appears in October, and which he sends out widely. He also meets the poet Marie Eugenie Delle Grazie and writes "Nature and Our Ideals" for her. He attends her salon, where he meets many priests, theologians, and philosophers, who will become his friends. Meanwhile, the director of the Goethe Archive in Weimar requests his collaboration with the *Sophien* edition of Goethe's works, particularly the writings on color.

1887: At the beginning of the year, Rudolf Steiner is very sick. As the year progresses and his health improves, he becomes increasingly "a man of letters," lecturing, writing essays, and taking part in Austrian cultural life. In August-September, the second volume of Goethe's *Scientific Writings* appears.

1888: January-July: Rudolf Steiner assumes editorship of the "German Weekly" (*Deutsche Wochenschrift*). He begins lecturing more intensively, giving, for example, a lecture titled "Goethe as Father of a New Aesthetics." He meets and becomes soul friends with Friedrich Eckstein (1861-1939), a vegetarian, philosopher of symbolism, alchemist, and musician, who will introduce him to various spiritual currents (including Theosophy) and with whom he will meditate and interpret esoteric and alchemical texts.

1889: Rudolf Steiner first reads Nietzsche (*Beyond Good and Evil*). He encounters Theosophy again and learns of Madame Blavatsky in the Theosophical circle around Marie Lang (1858-1934). Here he also meets well-known figures of Austrian life, as well as esoteric figures like the occultist Franz Hartman and Karl Leinigen-Billigen (translator of C.G. Harrison's *The Transcendental Universe*.) During this period, Steiner first reads A.P. Sinnett's *Esoteric Buddhism* and Mabel Collins's *Light on the Path*. He also begins traveling, visiting Budapest, Weimar, and Berlin (where he meets philosopher Edouard von Hartman).

1890: Rudolf Steiner finishes volume 3 of Goethe's scientific writings. He begins his doctoral dissertation, which will become *Truth and Science* (CW 3). He also meets the poet and feminist Rosa Mayreder (1858-1938), with whom he can exchange his most intimate thoughts. In September, Rudolf Steiner moves to Weimar to work in the Goethe-Schiller Archive.

1891: Volume 3 of the Kurschner edition of Goethe appears. Meanwhile, Rudolf Steiner edits Goethe's studies in mineralogy and scientific writings for the *Sophien* edition. He meets Ludwig Laistner of the Cotta Publishing Company, who asks for a book on the basic question of metaphysics. From this will result, ultimately, *The Philosophy of Freedom* (CW 4), which will be published not by Cotta but by Emil Felber. In October, Rudolf Steiner takes the oral exam for a doctorate in philosophy, mathematics, and mechanics at Rostock University, receiving his doctorate on the twenty-sixth. In November, he gives his first lecture on Goethe's "Fairy Tale" in Vienna.

1892: Rudolf Steiner continues work at the Goethe-Schiller Archive and on his *Philosophy of Freedom*. *Truth and Science*, his doctoral dissertation, is published. Steiner undertakes to write introductions to books on Schopenhauer and Jean Paul for Cotta. At year's end, he finds lodging with Anna Eunike, née Schulz (1853-1911), a widow with four daughters and a son. He also develops a friendship with Otto Erich Hartleben (1864-1905) with whom he shares literary interests.

1893: Rudolf Steiner begins his habit of producing many reviews and articles. In March, he gives a lecture titled "Hypnotism, with Reference to Spiritism." In September, volume 4 of the Kurschner edition is completed. In November, *The Philosophy of Freedom* appears. This year, too, he meets John Henry Mackay (1864-1933), the anarchist, and Max Stirner, a scholar and biographer.

1894: Rudolf Steiner meets Elisabeth Förster Nietzsche, the philosopher's sister, and begins to read Nietzsche in earnest, beginning with the as yet unpublished *Antichrist.* He also meets Ernst Haeckel (1834-1919). In the fall, he begins to write *Nietzsche, A Fighter against His Time* (CW 5).

1895: May, *Nietzsche, A Fighter against His Time* appears.

1896: January 22: Rudolf Steiner sees Friedrich Nietzsche for the first and only time. Moves between the Nietzsche and the Goethe-Schiller Archives, where he completes his work before year's end. He falls out with Elisabeth Förster Nietzsche, thus ending his association with the Nietzsche Archive.

1897: Rudolf Steiner finishes the manuscript of *Goethe's Worldview* (CW 6). He moves to Berlin with Anna Eunike and begins editorship of the *Magazin fur Literatur.* From now on, Steiner will write countless reviews, literary and philosophical articles, and so on. He begins lecturing at the "Free Literary Society." In September, he attends the Zionist Congress in Basel. He sides with Dreyfus in the Dreyfus affair.

1898: Rudolf Steiner is very active as an editor in the political, artistic, and theatrical life of Berlin. He becomes friendly with John Henry Mackay and poet Ludwig Jacobowski (1868-1900). He joins Jacobowski's circle of writers, artists, and scientists—"The Coming Ones" (*Die Kommenden*)—and contributes lectures to the group until 1903. He also lectures at the "League for College Pedagogy." He writes an article for Goethe's sesquicentennial, "Goethe's Secret Revelation," on the "Fairy Tale of the Green Snake and the Beautiful Lily."

1898-99: "This was a trying time for my soul as I looked at Christianity. . . . I was able to progress only by contemplating, by means of spiritual perception, the evolution of Christianity . . . . Conscious knowledge of real Christianity began to dawn in me around the turn of the century. This seed continued to develop. My soul trial occurred shortly before the beginning of the twentieth century. It was decisive for my soul's development that I stood spiritually before the Mystery of Golgotha in a deep and solemn celebration of knowledge."

1899: Rudolf Steiner begins teaching and giving lectures and lecture cycles at the Workers' College, founded by Wilhelm Liebknecht (1826-1900). He will continue to do so until 1904. Writes: *Literature and Spiritual Life in the Nineteenth Century; Individualism in Philosophy; Haeckel and His Opponents; Poetry in the Present;* and begins what will become (fifteen years later). *The Riddles of Philosophy* (CW 18). He also meets many artists and writers, including Käthe Kollwitz, Stefan

Zweig, and Rainer Maria Rilke. On October 31, he marries Anna Eunike.

1900: "I thought that the turn of the century must bring humanity a new light. It seemed to me that the separation of human thinking and willing from the spirit had peaked. A turn or reversal of direction in human evolution seemed to me a necessity." Rudolf Steiner finishes *World and Life Views in the Nineteenth Century* (the second part of what will become *The Riddles of Philosophy*) and dedicates it to Ernst Haeckel. It is published in March. He continues lecturing at *Die Kommenden*, whose leadership he assumes after the death of Jacobowski. Also, he gives the Gutenberg Jubilee lecture before 7,000 typesetters and printers. In September, Rudolf Steiner is invited by Count and Countess Brockdorff to lecture in the Theosophical Library. His first lecture is on Nietzsche. His second lecture is titled "Goethe's Secret Revelation." October 6, he begins a lecture cycle on the mystics that will become *Mystics after Modernism* (CW 7). November-December: "Marie von Sivers appears in the audience...." Also in November, Steiner gives his first lecture at the Giordano Bruno Bund (where he will continue to lecture until May, 1905). He speaks on Bruno and modern Rome, focusing on the importance of the philosophy of Thomas Aquinas as monism.

1901: In continual financial straits, Rudolf Steiner's early friends Moritz Zitter and Rosa Mayreder help support him. In October, he begins the lecture cycle *Christianity as Mystical Fact* (CW 8) at the Theosophical Library. In November, he gives his first "Theosophical lecture" on Goethe's "Fairy Tale" in Hamburg at the invitation of Wilhelm Hubbe-Schleiden. He also attends a tea to celebrate the founding of the Theosophical Society at Count and Countess Brockdorff's. He gives a lecture cycle, "From Buddha to Christ," for the circle of the *Kommenden*. November 17, Marie von Sivers asks Rudolf Steiner if Theosophy does not need a Western-Christian spiritual movement (to complement Theosophy's Eastern emphasis). "The question was posed. Now, following spiritual laws, I could begin to give an answer...." In December, Rudolf Steiner writes his first article for a Theosophical publication. At year's end, the Brockdorffs and possibly Wilhelm Hubbe-Schleiden ask Rudolf Steiner to join the Theosophical Society and undertake the leadership of the German section. Rudolf Steiner agrees, on the condition that Marie von Sivers (then in Italy) work with him.

1902: Beginning in January, Rudolf Steiner attends the opening of the Workers' School in Spandau with Rosa Luxemberg (1870-1919). January 17, Rudolf Steiner joins the Theosophical Society. In April, he is asked to become general secretary of the German Section of the Theosophical Society, and works on preparations for its founding. In July, he visits London for a Theosophical congress. He meets Bertram

Keightly, G.R.S. Mead, A.P. Sinnett, and Annie Besant, among others. In September, *Christianity as Mystical Fact* appears. In October, Rudolf Steiner gives his first public lecture on Theosophy ("Monism and Theosophy") to about three hundred people at the Giordano Bruno Bund. On October 19-21, the German Section of the Theosophical Society has its first meeting; Rudolf Steiner is the general secretary, and Annie Besant attends. Steiner lectures on practical karma studies. On October 23, Annie Besant inducts Rudolf Steiner into the Esoteric School of the Theosophical Society. On October 25, Steiner begins a weekly series of lectures: "The Field of Theosophy." During this year, Rudolf Steiner also first meets Ita Wegman (1876-1943), who will become his close collaborator in his final years.

1903: Rudolf Steiner holds about 300 lectures and seminars. In May, the first issue of the periodical *Luzifer* appears. In June, Rudolf Steiner visits London for the first meeting of the Federation of the European Sections of the Theosophical Society, where he meets Colonel Olcott. He begins to write *Theosophy* (CW 9).

1904: Rudolf Steiner continues lecturing at the Workers' College and elsewhere (about 90 lectures), while lecturing intensively all over Germany among Theosophists (about a 140 lectures). In February, he meets Carl Unger (1878-1929), who will become a member of the board of the Anthroposophical Society (1913). In March, he meets Michael Bauer (1871-1929), a Christian mystic, who will also be on the board. In May, *Theosophy* appears, with the dedication: "To the spirit of Giordano Bruno." Rudolf Steiner and Marie von Sivers visit London for meetings with Annie Besant. June: Rudolf Steiner and Marie von Sivers attend the meeting of the Federation of European Sections of the Theosophical Society in Amsterdam. In July, Steiner begins the articles in *Luzifer-Gnosis* that will become *How to Know Higher Worlds* (CW 10) and *Cosmic Memory* (CW 11). In September, Annie Besant visits Germany. In December, Steiner lectures on Freemasonry. He mentions the High Grade Masonry derived from John Yarker and represented by Theodore Reuss and Karl Kellner as a blank slate "into which a good image could be placed."

1905: This year, Steiner ends his non-Theosophical lecturing activity. Supported by Marie von Sivers, his Theosophical lecturing—both in public and in the Theosophical Society—increases significantly: "The German Theosophical Movement is of exceptional importance." Steiner recommends reading, among others, Fichte, Jacob Boehme, and Angelus Silesius. He begins to introduce Christian themes into Theosophy. He also begins to work with doctors (Felix Peipers and Ludwig Noll). In July, he is in London for the Federation of European Sections, where he attends a lecture by Annie Besant: "I have seldom seen Mrs. Besant speak in so inward and heartfelt a manner...." "Through Mrs. Besant I have found the way to H.P. Blavatsky."

September to October, he gives a course of thirty-one lectures for a small group of esoteric students. In October, the annual meeting of the German Section of the Theosophical Society, which still remains very small, takes place. Rudolf Steiner reports membership has risen from 121 to 377 members. In November, seeking to establish esoteric "continuity," Rudolf Steiner and Marie von Sivers participate in a "Memphis-Misraim" Masonic ceremony. They pay forty-five marks for membership. "Yesterday, you saw how little remains of former esoteric institutions." "We are dealing only with a 'framework'... for the present, nothing lies behind it. The occult powers have completely withdrawn."

1906: Expansion of Theosophical work. Rudolf Steiner gives about 245 lectures, only 44 of which take place in Berlin. Cycles are given in Paris, Leipzig, Stuttgart, and Munich. Esoteric work also intensifies. Rudolf Steiner begins writing *An Outline of Esoteric Science* (CW 13). In January, Rudolf Steiner receives permission (a patent) from the Great Orient of the Scottish A & A Thirty-Three Degree Rite of the Order of the Ancient Freemasons of the Memphis-Misraim Rite to direct a chapter under the name "Mystica Aeterna." This will become the "Cognitive Cultic Section" (also called "Misraim Service") of the Esoteric School. (See: *From the History and Contents of the Cognitive Cultic Section* (CW 264). During this time, Steiner also meets Albert Schweitzer. In May, he is in Paris, where he visits Edouard Schuré. Many Russians attend his lectures (including Konstantin Balmont, Dimitri Mereszkovski, Zinaida Hippius, and Maximilian Woloshin). He attends the General Meeting of the European Federation of the Theosophical Society, at which Col. Olcott is present for the last time. He spends the year's end in Venice and Rome, where he writes and works on his translation of H.P. Blavatsky's *Key to Theosophy.*

1907: Further expansion of the German Theosophical Movement according to the Rosicrucian directive to "introduce spirit into the world"—in education, in social questions, in art, and in science. In February, Col. Olcott dies in Adyar. Before he dies, Olcott indicates that "the Masters" wish Annie Besant to succeed him: much politicking ensues. Rudolf Steiner supports Besant's candidacy. April-May: preparations for the Congress of the Federation of European Sections of the Theosophical Society—the great, watershed Whitsun "Munich Congress," attended by Annie Besant and others. Steiner decides to separate Eastern and Western (Christian-Rosicrucian) esoteric schools. He takes his esoteric school out of the Theosophical Society (Besant and Rudolf Steiner are "in harmony" on this). Steiner makes his first lecture tours to Austria and Hungary. That summer, he is in Italy. In September, he visits Edouard Schuré, who will write the introduction to the French edition of *Christianity as Mystical Fact* in Barr, Alsace. Rudolf Steiner writes the autobiographical statement known as the "Barr Document." In *Luzifer-Gnosis,* "The Education of the Child" appears.

1908: The movement grows (membership: 1150). Lecturing expands. Steiner makes his first extended lecture tour to Holland and Scandinavia, as well as visits to Naples and Sicily. Themes: St. John's Gospel, the Apocalypse, Egypt, science, philosophy, and logic. *Luzifer-Gnosis* ceases publication. In Berlin, Marie von Sivers (with Johanna Mücke (1864-1949) forms the *Philosophisch-Theosophisch* (after 1915 *Philosophisch-Anthroposophisch*) *Verlag* to publish Steiner's work. Steiner gives lecture cycles titled *The Gospel of St. John* (CW 103) and *The Apocalypse* (104).

1909: *An Outline of Esoteric Science* appears. Lecturing and travel continues. Rudolf Steiner's spiritual research expands to include the polarity of Lucifer and Ahriman; the work of great individualities in history; the Maitreya Buddha and the Bodhisattvas; spiritual economy (CW 109); the work of the spiritual hierarchies in heaven and on Earth (CW 110). He also deepens and intensifies his research into the Gospels, giving lectures on the Gospel of St. Luke (CW 114) with the first mention of two Jesus children. Meets and becomes friends with Christian Morgenstern (1871-1914). In April, he lays the foundation stone for the Malsch model—the building that will lead to the first Goetheanum. In May, the International Congress of the Federation of European Sections of the Theosophical Society takes place in Budapest. Rudolf Steiner receives the Subba Row medal for *How to Know Higher Worlds*. During this time, Charles W. Leadbeater discovers Jiddu Krishnamurti (1895-1986) and proclaims him the future "world teacher," the bearer of the Maitreya Buddha and the "reappearing Christ." In October, Steiner delivers seminal lectures on "anthroposophy," which he will try, unsuccessfully, to rework over the next years into the unfinished work, *Anthroposophy (A Fragment)* (CW 45).

1910: New themes: *The Reappearance of Christ in the Etheric* (CW 118); *The Fifth Gospel; The Mission of Folk Souls* (CW 121); *Occult History* (CW 126); the evolving development of etheric cognitive capacities. Rudolf Steiner continues his Gospel research with *The Gospel of St. Matthew* (CW 123). In January, his father dies. In April, he takes a month-long trip to Italy, including Rome, Monte Cassino, and Sicily. He also visits Scandinavia again. July-August, he writes the first mystery drama, *The Portal of Initiation* (CW 14). In November, he gives "psychosophy" lectures. In December, he submits "On the Psychological Foundations and Epistemological Framework of Theosophy" to the International Philosophical Congress in Bologna.

1911: The crisis in the Theosophical Society deepens. In January, "The Order of the Rising Sun," which will soon become "The Order of the Star in the East," is founded for the coming world teacher, Krishnamurti. At the same time, Marie von Sivers, Rudolf Steiner's coworker, falls ill. Fewer lectures are given, but important new ground is broken. In Prague, in March, Steiner meets Franz Kafka (1883-1924) and Hugo Bergmann (1883-1975). In April, he delivers his paper to the

Philosophical Congress. He writes the second mystery drama, *The Soul's Probation* (CW 14). Also, while Marie von Sivers is convalescing, Rudolf Steiner begins work on *Calendar 1912/1913*, which will contain the "Calendar of the Soul" meditations. On March 19, Anna (Eunike) Steiner dies. In September, Rudolf Steiner visits Einsiedeln, birthplace of Paracelsus. In December, Friedrich Rittelmeyer, future founder of the Christian Community, meets Rudolf Steiner. The *Johannes-Bauverein*, the "building committee," which would lead to the first Goetheanum (first planned for Munich), is also founded, and a preliminary committee for the founding of an independent association is created that, in the following year, will become the Anthroposophical Society. Important lecture cycles include *Occult Physiology* (CW 128); *Wonders of the World* (CW 129); *From Jesus to Christ* (CW 131). Other themes: esoteric Christianity; Christian Rosenkreutz; the spiritual guidance of humanity; the sense world and the world of the spirit.

1912: Despite the ongoing, now increasing crisis in the Theosophical Society, much is accomplished: *Calendar 1912/1913* is published; eurythmy is created; both the third mystery drama, *The Guardian of the Threshold* (CW 14) and *A Way of Self-Knowledge* (CW 16) are written. New (or renewed) themes included life between death and rebirth and karma and reincarnation. Other lecture cycles: *Spiritual Beings in the Heavenly Bodies and the Kingdoms of Nature* (CW 136); *The Human Being in the Light of Occultism, Theosophy, and Philosophy* (CW 137); *The Gospel of St. Mark* (CW 139); and *The Bhagavad Gita and the Epistles of Paul* (CW 142). On May 8, Rudolf Steiner celebrates White Lotus Day, H.P. Blavatsky's death day, which he had faithfully observed for the past decade, for the last time. In August, Rudolf Steiner suggests the "independent association" be called the "Anthroposophical Society." In September, the first eurythmy course takes place. In October, Rudolf Steiner declines recognition of a Theosophical Society lodge dedicated to the Star of the East and decides to expel all Theosophical Society members belonging to the order. Also, with Marie von Sivers, he first visits Dornach, near Basel, Switzerland, and they stand on the hill where the Goetheanum will be. In November, a Theosophical Society lodge is opened by direct mandate from Adyar (Annie Besant). In December, a meeting of the German section occurs at which it is decided that belonging to the Order of the Star of the East is incompatible with membership in the Theosophical Society. December 28: informal founding of the Anthroposophical Society in Berlin.

1913: Expulsion of the German section from the Theosophical Society. February 2-3: Foundation meeting of the Anthroposophical Society. Board members include: Marie von Sivers, Michael Bauer, and Carl Unger. September 20: Laying of the foundation stone for the *Johannes Bau* (Goetheanum) in Dornach. Building begins immediately. The third mystery drama, *The Soul's Awakening* (CW 14), is completed.

Also: *The Threshold of the Spiritual World* (CW 147). Lecture cycles include: *The Bhagavad Gita and the Epistles of Paul* and *The Esoteric Meaning of the Bhagavad Gita* (CW 146), which the Russian philosopher Nikolai Berdyaev attends; *The Mysteries of the East and of Christianity* (CW 144); *The Effects of Esoteric Development* (CW 145); and *The Fifth Gospel* (CW 148). In May, Rudolf Steiner is in London and Paris, where anthroposophical work continues.

1914: Building continues on the *Johannes Bau* (Goetheanum) in Dornach, with artists and coworkers from seventeen nations. The general assembly of the Anthroposophical Society takes place. In May, Rudolf Steiner visits Paris, as well as Chartres Cathedral. June 28: assassination in Sarajevo ("Now the catastrophe has happened!"). August 1: War is declared. Rudolf Steiner returns to Germany from Dornach—he will travel back and forth. He writes the last chapter of *The Riddles of Philosophy*. Lecture cycles include: *Human and Cosmic Thought* (CW 151); *Inner Being of Humanity between Death and a New Birth* (CW 153); *Occult Reading and Occult Hearing* (CW 156). December 24: marriage of Rudolf Steiner and Marie von Sivers.

1915: Building continues. Life after death becomes a major theme, also art. Writes: *Thoughts during a Time of War* (CW 24). Lectures include: *The Secret of Death* (CW 159); *The Uniting of Humanity through the Christ Impulse* (CW 165).

1916: Rudolf Steiner begins work with Edith Maryon (1872-1924) on the sculpture "The Representative of Humanity" ("The Group"—Christ, Lucifer, and Ahriman). He also works with the alchemist Alexander von Bernus on the quarterly *Das Reich*. He writes *The Riddle of Humanity* (CW 20). Lectures include: *Necessity and Freedom in World History and Human Action* (CW 166); *Past and Present in the Human Spirit* (CW 167); *The Karma of Vocation* (CW 172); *The Karma of Untruthfulness* (CW 173).

1917: Russian Revolution. The U.S. enters the war. Building continues. Rudolf Steiner delineates the idea of the "threefold nature of the human being" (in a public lecture March 15) and the "threefold nature of the social organism" (hammered out in May-June with the help of Otto von Lerchenfeld and Ludwig Polzer-Hoditz in the form of two documents titled *Memoranda*, which were distributed in high places). August-September: Rudolf Steiner writes *The Riddles of the Soul* (CW 20). Also: commentary on "The Chemical Wedding of Christian Rosenkreutz" for Alexander Bernus (*Das Reich*). Lectures include: *The Karma of Materialism* (CW 176); *The Spiritual Background of the Outer World: The Fall of the Spirits of Darkness* (CW 177).

1918: March 18: peace treaty of Brest-Litovsk—"Now everything will truly enter chaos! What is needed is cultural renewal." June: Rudolf Steiner visits Karlstein (Grail) Castle outside Prague. Lecture cycle: *From Symptom to Reality in Modern History* (CW 185). In mid-November,

Emil Molt, of the Waldorf-Astoria Cigarette Company, has the idea of founding a school for his workers' children.

1919: Focus on the threefold social organism: tireless travel, countless lectures, meetings, and publications. At the same time, a new public stage of Anthroposophy emerges as cultural renewal begins. The coming years will see initiatives in pedagogy, medicine, pharmacology, and agriculture. January 27: threefold meeting: "We must first of all, with the money we have, found free schools that can bring people what they need." February: first public eurythmy performance in Zurich. Also: "Appeal to the German People" (CW 24), circulated March 6 as a newspaper insert. In April, *Toward Social Renewal* (CW 23)—"perhaps the most widely read of all books on politics appearing since the war"—appears. Rudolf Steiner is asked to undertake the "direction and leadership" of the school founded by the Waldorf-Astoria Company. Rudolf Steiner begins to talk about the "renewal" of education. May 30: a building is selected and purchased for the future Waldorf School. August-September, Rudolf Steiner gives a lecture course for Waldorf teachers, *The Foundations of Human Experience (Study of Man)* (CW 293). September 7: Opening of the first Waldorf School. December (into January): first science course, the *Light Course* (CW 320).

1920: The Waldorf School flourishes. New threefold initiatives. Founding of limited companies *Der Kommenden Tag* and *Futurum A.G.* to infuse spiritual values into the economic realm. Rudolf Steiner also focuses on the sciences. Lectures: *Introducing Anthroposophical Medicine* (CW 312); *The Warmth Course* (CW 321); *The Boundaries of Natural Science* (CW 322); *The Redemption of Thinking* (CW 74). February: Johannes Werner Klein—later a cofounder of the Christian Community—asks Rudolf Steiner about the possibility of a "religious renewal," a "Johannine church." In March, Rudolf Steiner gives the first course for doctors and medical students. In April, a divinity student asks Rudolf Steiner a second time about the possibility of religious renewal. September 27-October 16: anthroposophical "university course." December: lectures titled *The Search for the New Isis* (CW 202).

1921: Rudolf Steiner continues his intensive work on cultural renewal, including the uphill battle for the threefold social order. "University" arts, scientific, theological, and medical courses include: *The Astronomy Course* (CW 323); *Observation, Mathematics, and Scientific Experiment* (CW 324); the *Second Medical Course* (CW 313); *Color* (CW 291). In June and September-October, Rudolf Steiner also gives the first two "priests' courses" (CW 342 and 343). The "youth movement" gains momentum. Magazines are founded: *Die Drei* (January), and—under the editorship of Albert Steffen (1884-1963)—the weekly, *Das Goetheanum* (August). In February-March, Rudolf Steiner takes his first trip outside Germany since the war (Holland). On April 7, Steiner receives a letter regarding "religious renewal," and May 22-23, he agrees to address the question in a practical way. In June, the Klinical-Therapeutic Institute opens in Arlesheim under the direction of Dr. Ita Wegman. In August, the Chemical-Pharmaceutical Laboratory opens in Arlesheim (Oskar Schmiedel and Ita Wegman, directors). The Clinical Therapeutic Institute is inaugurated in Stuttgart (Dr. Ludwig Noll, director); also the Research Laboratory in Dornach (Ehrenfried Pfeiffer and Gunther Wachsmuth, directors). In November-December, Rudolf Steiner visits Norway.

1922: The first half of the year involves very active public lecturing (thousands attend); in the second half, Rudolf Steiner begins to withdraw and turn toward the Society—"The Society is asleep." It is "too weak" to do what is asked of it. The businesses—*Die Kommenden Tag* and *Futura A.G.*—fail. In January, with the help of an agent, Steiner undertakes a twelve-city German tour, accompanied by eurythmy performances. In two weeks he speaks to more than 2,000 people. In April, he gives a "university course" in The Hague. He also visits England. In June, he is in Vienna for the East-West Congress. In August-September, he is back in England for the Oxford Conference on Education. Returning to Dornach, he gives the lectures *Philosophy, Cosmology, and Religion* (CW 215), and gives the third priest's course (CW 344). On September 16, The Christian Community is founded. In October-November, Steiner is in Holland and England. He also speaks to the youth: *Becoming Michael's Companions* (CW 217). In December, Steiner gives lectures titled *The Origins of Natural Science* (CW 326), and *Humanity and the World of Stars: The Spiritual Communion of Humanity* (CW 219). December 31: Fire at the Goetheanum, which is destroyed.

1923: Despite the fire, Rudolf Steiner continues his work unabated. A very hard year. Internal dispersion, dissension, and apathy abound. There is conflict—between old and new visions—within the society. A wake-up call is needed, and Rudolf Steiner responds with renewed lecturing vitality. His focus: the spiritual context of human life; initiation science; the course of the year; and community building. As a foundation for an artistic school, he creates a series of pastel sketches. Lecture cycles: *The Anthroposophical Movement; Initiation Science* (CW 227) (in England at the Penmaenmawr Summer School); *The Four Seasons and the Archangels* (CW 229); *Harmony of the Creative Word* (CW 230); *The Supersensible Human* (CW 231), given in Holland for the founding of the Dutch society. On November 10, in response to the failed Hitler-Ludendorf putsch in Munich, Steiner closes his Berlin residence and moves the *Philosophisch-Anthroposophisch Verlag* (Press) to Dornach. On December 9, Steiner begins the serialization of his *Autobiography: The Course of My Life* (CW 28) in *Das Goetheanum*. It will continue to appear weekly, without a break, until his death. Late December-early January: Rudolf Steiner refounds the Anthroposophical Society (about

12,000 members internationally) and takes over its leadership. The new board members are: Marie Steiner, Ita Wegman, Albert Steffen, Elizabeth Vreede, and Guenther Wachsmuth. (See *The Christmas Meeting for the Founding of the General Anthro-posophical Society* (CW 260). Accompanying lectures: *Mystery Knowledge and Mystery Centers* (CW 232); *World History in the Light of Anthroposophy* (CW 233). December 25: the Foundation Stone is laid (in the hearts of members) in the form of the "Foundation Stone Meditation."

1924: January 1: having founded the Anthroposophical Society and taken over its leadership, Rudolf Steiner has the task of "reforming" it. The process begins with a weekly newssheet ("What's Happening in the Anthroposophical Society") in which Rudolf Steiner's "Letters to Members" and "Anthroposophical Leading Thoughts" appear (CW 26). The next step is the creation of a new esoteric class, the "first class" of the "University of Spiritual Science" (which was to have been followed, had Rudolf Steiner lived longer, by two more advanced classes). Then comes a new language for Anthroposophy—practical, phenomenological, and direct; and Rudolf Steiner creates the model for the second Goetheanum. He begins the series of extensive "karma" lectures (CW 235-40); and finally, responding to needs, he creates two new initiatives: biodynamic agriculture and curative education. After the middle of the year, rumors begin to circulate regarding Steiner's health. Lectures: January-February, *Anthroposophy* (CW 234); February: *Tone Eurythmy* (CW 278); June: *The Agriculture Course* (CW 327); June-July: Speech [?] Eurythmy (CW 279); *Curative Education* (CW 317); August: (England, "Second International Summer School"), *Initiation Consciousness: True and False Paths in Spiritual Investigation* (CW 243); September: *Pastoral Medicine* (CW 318). On September 26, for the first time, Rudolf Steiner cancels a lecture. On September 28, he gives his last lecture. On September 29, he withdraws to his studio in the carpenter's shop; now he is definitively ill. Cared for by Ita Wegman, he continues working, however, and writing the weekly installments of his *Autobiography* and *Letters to the Members/Leading Thoughts* (CW 26).

1925: Rudolf Steiner, while continuing to work, continues to weaken. He finishes *Extending Practical Medicine* (CW 27) with Ita Wegman.

On March 30, around ten in the morning, Rudolf Steiner dies.

INDEX